STORIES & ESSAYS

JAN SEALE

LITERARY PRESS
LAMAR UNIVERSITY

ISBN: 978-1-942956-47-1
Library of Congress Control Number: 2017953322

Cover design and author photograph: Erren Seale
Book design: Salena Parker
Manufactured in the United States of America

Lamar University Literary Press
Beaumont, Texas

About Jan Seale's Writing

"I was struck by the unbroken thread of genuine wonder in the world, an unfolding of its little miracles with deft, certain metaphors."
—David Bowles, *The Monitor*

"Love for all things permeates Ms. Seale's vision always allowing, of course, for an alert sense of the ridiculous which can bring a laugh on just about any page."
—Laura Kennelly, *Texas Books in Review*

"Seale's meditations on chores, labors, and duties emphasize ritual rather than repetition or drudgery and in her lines the transcendent becomes visible."
—Jerry Bradley, *Concho River Review*

"A natural storyteller, her poems are both carefully crafted and wildly free wise evocations of nature, satiric takes on teaching writing and intimate narratives about family and friends (dead serious and endearing but never sentimental)."
—Robert Bonazzi, *The San Antonio Express-News*

"Seale's work displays her ability to hone in on the interiority of her characters' lives. *Appearances* is a graceful collection of the struggles and pleasures that reflect our shared humanity."
—Dena Garcia, *Texas Books in Review*

"Seale demonstrates a remarkable gift for addressing life's most difficult issues in a serious manner, yet using wry humor to leave the reader with a sense of hope."
—P.P.T., *The Baylor Line*

"Throughout these always whimsical essays, stuff so common we don't notice it becomes the basis for human struggle and dignity."
—Jim Sanderson, *Texas Writers Newsletter*

"The eighteen stories in *Airlift* will alternately lift your spirits and make you teary-eyed. Seale reveals the importance of trampolines and sewing machines and custom designed tombstones with a voice that is never condescending and always a pleasure to read."
—Melanie Alberts, *Story Circle Journal*

"What is particularly fine about this collection of poems is the steady presence of the voice, the clarity of its pitch.
—Patricia Grant, *The Monitor*

"Seale often pairs form and content ironically to jaw-dropping effect. This offbeat combination of almost-epic catalog and almost-but-not-quite heroic verse generates a gritty humor that recurs throughout the text and leavens an experience potentially devastating for reader and writer alike.
—Carol Coffee Reposa, *The Mimeograph*

"Seale possesses a Chekovian ability to render people and events significant and memorable."
—Delores Washburn, *Western American Literature*

"*Homeland* is a charmer whose message will stick with you long after you've turned the last page."
—Judyth Rigler, *Texas Books*

"Seale's "Believing Is Seeing" is a powerful collection where the poet enters the internal landscape of desert and spirit to write poetry that is both self-revealing and mysterious."
—Ray Gonzalez, *The Bloomsbury Review*

"Ms. Seale's genius lies in her ability to penetrate her characters' minds and find a single, poignant point to make about their lives, something that made them the way they are, perhaps the same thing that makes all of us the way we are."
—Clay Reynolds, *The Dallas Morning News*

Acknowledgments

The author gratefully acknowledges the following publications for first publication of versions of some essays in this book:

A Cup of Comfort

Amarillo Bay

Folklore in Motion

Mom Writer's Literary Magazine

New Texas 12

Red Boots & Attitude

The Monitor

The National Parkinson's Association

The Town Crier

The Woman

Valleysong

Writing Texas

Other books by Jan Seale

Airlift
Appearances
Audie & Company
Bonds
Homeland
Jan Seale: New and Selected Poems
Nape
Nature Nurture Neither
Sharing the House
The Parkinson Poems
The Wonder Is
The Yin of It
Valley Ark

to the
Charm Bracelet Girls

Barbara, Beverly, Carolyn, Janis,
Patricia, Phyllis K.† and Phyllis S.

Other Nonfiction from Lamar University Literary Press

Ted L. Estess *Fishing Spirit Lake*
Dominique Inge, *A Garden on the Brazos: Green Thoughts in a Texas
      Garden*
Terry C. Maxwell, *Tales of a Journeyman Naturalist*
Jim McJunkin, *Deep Sleep*
Jeanetta Calhoun Mish, *Oklahomeland*
Steven Schroeder, *What's Love Got To Do With It? a city out of thin air*

For information on these and other
Lamar University Literary Press Books, go to
www.lamar.edu/literarypress

Maybe we're here only to say: house,
bridge, well, gate, jug, olive tree, window —
at most, pillar, tower ... but to say them, remember,
oh, to say them in a way that the things themselves
never dreamed of existing so intensely.

—Rainer Maria Rilke

CONTENTS

IV. Groundings

I. Whims

Round the Mulberry Bush

Today I found a long white hair woven into the sleeve of a silk dress bought to wear at my son's wedding. For a moment I was startled. How could this be? I checked the label: Made in China. Of course. It happened when a woman bent over a loom, tending the skeins as they became cloth. She is a widow. She has one son. She lives with him, his wife, their one child in a small apartment. Her name is...Li Ping—because I once knew a woman by that name.

In my first grade classroom at J. Frank McMurray Elementary School was a four-foot square wooden rack built of 1X4's with a screen fitted over it. Each fall, Miss Ruth Garvey filled it with silkworms: *Bombyx mori*. It never occurred to me where she got them; the box was loaded with caterpillars at the beginning of school. She also provided a painting easel and a reading corner. If you finished your seatwork, you could paint a big juicy picture or read a more interesting book. Or you could go look at the silkworms. Miss Garvey was a progressive teacher.

Once we passed her first grade, we were invited year after year to come back and gaze at Miss Garvey's silkworms. She would even remind us, if she saw us on the playground or in the hallway, that she was counting on us to come check their progress.

Miss Garvey never married. She lived with her father in a neat white Victorian house with a beckoning porch on a street that I traversed to school each day on bike or foot. Many's the time I ran up on Miss Garvey's porch, seeking sanctuary from a vicious chow dog or a couple of bullies. Her porch always *worked:* no one except the legitimate would dare mount Miss Garvey's porch.

My sister and I played a piano duet at Miss Garvey's father's 100th birthday celebration. In the middle of our rendition, Father Garvey bawled out, "When is this going to be over?" Too late, Miss Garvey rushed to his side and put her hand over his mouth. Shortly after that, my sister refused to play the piano anymore. I should have.

Miss Garvey's current first graders had dibs on caring for the silkworms. She regularly issued an urgent call for her students to bring mulberry leaves, though I think she had a secret bountiful supply from her backyard trees. Nevertheless, we faithfully brought the bulksome branches, fresh as possible, from our yards. Several times a day, it was possible to go stand at the frame and, after a moment, perceive with a delicious shock the vast quivering movement of mulberry leaves as the silkworms on the underside ate their voracious way through the day's supply. It was better than a magic show, and we could cause it just by our willingness to stand still and look.

A weekend would pass and on Monday morning Miss Garvey showed us proudly that small cocoons had begun to form from the sticky threading of the larvae. We weren't to touch, just look, at those hairy ellipsoids growing larger each day. Some morning, when we'd started to get bored with staring at silent gray cigar-shaped objects in a box, Miss Garvey, right after lunch count and with a mysterious smile on her face, would ask, "Has anyone seen the surprise yet?" Then she'd call us to gather around, where we'd watch one or two wet silkworm moths laboring mightily to exit their prison chambers.

I think that all the moths did not come out at once, like cicadas or May flies, but that we had a surprise every few days. And I do not recall what happened to the moths. Did Miss Garvey take them home? Did she release them outside? Did they flit around the box and finally die? What, then, was the lesson we learned, returning year after year to experience Miss Garvey's silkworms?

For me it wasn't any lofty spiritual or ecological object lesson. The larvae were redolent in distaste, silent greedy munchers. The cocoons were teasers, requiring agonizing patience not to touch, just look, day after long day. And the moths didn't last.

Nor am I sure Miss Garvey ever pointed out to us the fluid nature of the creature inside the cocoon. Did she tell us that when the larva had completely spun itself a covering, and was on its way to pupahood, that it became soup—yes, soup—completely liquid, for a while? And then, and only then, did the pupa begin to form?

What Miss Garvey did was to give us ownership of those silkworms. They were ours, forever and ever, because she had us wag mulberry branches to school for them and sprinkle water very gently into their enclosure. Because she compelled us to come back, year on end, even when we felt entirely superior to her baby first graders, to view her silkworms. She taught us the power of patient observation. She taught us that nature had its own timetable and its peculiar gifts. She made us *look* at something long enough to love it. Miss Garvey was confoundedly, eternally excited about silkworms —thus, so were we.

Li Ping, whose white hair came across the world embedded in my silk dress, I know that I wear this particular dress because of you, a poorly paid Chinese worker, a woman probably my age, one who has borne children, cooked morning meals, prayed at night before sleep.

If I grow still and think truthfully, I also understand that my pale silk 3-piece dress from Steinmart originated by the sacrifice of hundreds of silkworm pupae, killed by dipping them in hot water before processing their dried milky skeins—this, after each has blindly spun as much as 3,000 feet of silk thread. Advertising bills silk as natural fiber, like cotton or linen. I will be cool in it. If I am greatly sorry for Li Ping, and a little sorry for the silkworms, should I not also be sorry for the cotton stalk and the flax? Life feeds upon life.

Teresa of Avila used the silkworm in her "Interior Castle" to illustrate to her followers the complete enclosure of the soul, the sealing off of one's self from the pleasures of an exterior life in order to emerge as a higher being in the will of God.

So it is, that by a simple white hair, unnoticed, falling on to the loom over which a worker halfway around the world bends to achieve her daily quota, I come to a larger world.

We humans have our opposable thumb, our language, our tools. We also have our conscious will to remember.

Silkworms: Miss Garvey, Li Ping, St. Teresa and me. A barren maiden-lady school teacher, a middle-aged Chinese factory worker, a mystical sixteenth-century reformer, a mother of a groom...

Things really do go round, come round. Like larva equal cocoon equal pupa equal chrysalis equal moth. Like cocoon equal thread equal cloth equal wedding clothes.

Like stray hairs are links. Like memory of one's first grade teacher equals love passed on to bride and groom.

Held, bonded, we are all of us dressed in each other's silks, woven together across time and universe in a garment of existence that assures us we are not alone.

Scriptophobia and Other Nasty Fears

Okay, I have to get on with this piece about phobias, but I have a bit of scriptophobia, fear of writing. Whatever. With over 500 phobias listed on the Net, there's probably no one on earth without at least four or five. A phobia is an intense, persistent, illogical, abnormal or unnatural fear. Everyone, but everyone, even the psychologists who diagnose phobias no doubt have phobophobia, the fear of phobias. And why shouldn't we all have ballistophobia, fear of bullets, or taurophobia, fear of bulls? I don't know about you but I've had thanatophobia, fear of death, all my life.

Some just bear holding up to the light. There's pteronophobia, the fear of being tickled with feathers; alliumphobia, fear of garlic; and geniophobia, fear of chins. Then there's ranidaphobia, fear of frogs; xanthophobia, fear of the color yellow, and octophobia, fear of the figure eight.

I found myself especially interested in these two: aulophobia, fear of flutes; and metrophobia, fear of poetry. I'm a longtime flute player and I can just imagine giving my parents aulophobia when they heard unmusical squeaks coming from my bedroom. Metrophobia: a fear of poetry? I think I've seen that affliction on the faces of students forced, on pain of an F, to come to one of my poetry readings in a college auditorium.

Hydrophobia is in a class all its own. That's another name for rabies, since the poor victims cannot drink water because of muscle spasms, this being interpreted as their fear of water. Has hydrophobia lost credence in modern medical parlance? I seem to have heard it used more when I was a child.

As if over 500 phobias was not enough, I have invented a few myself, trying for some euphonious terms that will render the feared item near innocuous. There's stroganophobia, the fear of getting fat on noodles; Baryshnikophobia, the fear of being danced on; and miniaturegolphobia, the fear of waiting your turn. Then there's styrophobia, fear of portable ice chests; guffawphobia, fear of laughter; and foephobia, fear of enemies.

I once knew a woman who had a fear of stretch limos. She said they were *muy feo* (very ugly) and would shudder and turn her head if she saw one. I myself am far above such naiveté. Instead, I have a phobia about the dancing grape clusters on TV ads, a form of fructophobia. I have to avert my eyes when those hefty little purple globs bounce onto the screen, this until a fellow viewer gives me the all-okay sign.

The opposite of phobia is philia, the Greek word for brotherly love and often used to distinguish friendly love from sexual or godly love. Philia is a favorite of Bible-teaching folk. Think Philadelphia, the city of brotherly love.

The philia name comes from...of course...a Greek goddess named Philotes. She was the daughter of the goddess Nyx and personified affection, friendship, and sex. (Don't tell the Bible scholars.) In the broader sense, and attached to root words, -philia has come to mean any kind of allure, magnetism, or craving for another person or thing. If I had my druthers, I'd rather folks thought of me as having a philia rather than a phobia. Come to think of it, both sound a little extreme.

Air Talk

The Rio Grande Valley of Texas, where my home is, constitutes the jumping-off place for flights in the southern United States. This is a place where one can see contented rabbits hopping about on the grassy divider between runways. Once, an obviously weary flight attendant was delivering her final patter. "...and have a safe and pleasant journey to the city of your final destination." A pause. "Oh! This *is* your final destination."

We are a long way from the rest of civilization, so if I want to go anywhere, airline travel is the best means. Through the years, I've come to feel that flying is a storyteller's paradise. Your seat partner will tell you stories they've not told anyone else (or say they haven't). And you, in turn, may do some divulging yourself. It's a unique venue for psychiatric help, autobiography, confession, and celebration.

I wish I could know how the lives of all my airplane seat partners have turned out. Like Chuckie, the eight year old traveling between divorced parents. He had a book and a snack of cheese and crackers in his backpack and kept struggling with his too large ID badge. He flew a round trip of this route every Saturday between Houston and the Rio Grande Valley. Is he a confident sixteen year old now, with good grades and a girlfriend? Or is he a mess, full of angst and self-doubt for the weekly disruption of his life?

How about the Cuban man who spoke into my ear in Ricky Ricardo accent as we admired the earth's patterns out the window, "The earth is awesome. It is the most beautiful thing God has given us beside the animals and the opposite sex."

Or the forester from my hometown who told me how to help my blind neighbor plant an appropriate tree in his yard that would give him shade before he died.

I didn't step into an airplane until I was 35 years old. Now over twice that age, as a designated frequent flyer by two airlines, I find my on-board activity is a toss-up between a window seat where I can admire the terrain, and being lucky enough to have a fascinating seat partner.

I am addicted to the life stories people disclose on flights. There are dry narratives, rants and raves, stories of love and coincidence, bits of wisdom, pronouncements of opinions and druthers. Why I thrill and thrive on all this, I don't exactly know. I don't often use these stories in my writing. I certainly don't agree with many of the sentiments. I might find them boring if I had to sit all afternoon or evening on a front porch and hear these people talk. But a flight—now that's different. We are all crammed in a metal tube zooming across an oxygen-thin atmosphere at an average of 567 miles an hour. Touch-down will be in one hour and twenty-six minutes. What exchanges can happen in that time? I will be different when I deplane.

I must admit that on longer flights I have to rein in my curiosity, listen a while and then excuse myself with a magazine. Otherwise, I won't be able to communicate properly when I get to my destination. I'll be too jazzed with the exotic stories, the incredible variety of lives that chance has placed me with.

Travel brings out family stories. People are going to funerals or weddings or reunions. For example, Hazel Smith of Jackson, Miss. was going to the wedding of a grandchild. Hazel planned to wear white. Did I think that was wrong?

They often begin to reminisce or bring up old hurts, things they can divulge to a stranger and be rid of—at least for a little while—when they get to their destination. Take the man who told me his father had been married three times without bothering to divorce the first two wives. My seat partner went to his father's deathbed and asked him very politely, "Are you right with the Lord?" The father replied, "Get out!" The son didn't bother to go to his father's funeral. Now, now his grandchild has been born with hydroencephalitis and has a shunt in his head. All I can do is shake my head and say, "*Lo siento* (I'm sorry)."

Or the woman who explained in some detail the genesis and exodus of her diamond rings. Ah, the stories behind those blings!

A lady whose mother had a gall bladder operation was taking her a wooden rose, which she couched carefully in her hands.

Once, as we were getting settled before take-off, we overheard a loud cell phone monolog from a woman hefting her carryon into the overhead: "I'm going to tell you something in strictest confidence, and if you ever tell anyone...Oh, are you there?" We were, all ears, when she turned to us accusingly and bellowed, "Dammit! My cell phone just went out."

A blonde, blue-eyed college coed was chagrined because she had forgotten her mousse. I wanted to show her a patch of ground like a Navajo rug but she was reading "Anatomy of a Breakup." Her breath smelled faintly acidic, the result of a long bout with braces. Her responses were "cool," "awesome," "sick!" and "oooh." Everything was so "something," her quoted dialogs punctuated with "she goes" and "I go."

I once asked if I could sit by a pleasant woman of normal weight. (You have to be careful these days choosing your seatmates because, as one airline puts it, there are "customers of size.") As this nice-looking lady was assenting, she broke into a broad grin. It seems that months earlier, I had asked the same question, and she had said yes then also. We knew some of the same people so we picked up where we left off.

Then, there was a man who turned out to be my dentist's relative. He wanted to tell me what he had discovered about vitamin D.

The one-world concept is never better illustrated than among airline passengers. I remember the part-Indian insurance salesman from Milwaukee, the priest from Brazil, the California lady who will pray for me, the CPA from Dallas who can't wait to get home to his five daughters, the Jewish businessman from the Bronx who thinks he is going to take a rented car across the border into Mexico, the Oregon woman longing for her cabin on a lake, the Russian who likes New Jersey better than New York, the Mexican pilot of small planes who is on a romantic prowl.

I relish the philosophies spoken: "There are two kinds of women. One is the one who learns early that women and men are totally different and the other kind is the one who thinks we all start out even and then learns better and the hard way."

Where else could I get a patient explanation over and over from a nuclear physicist on how safe the 18-passenger short carrier was in a rainstorm over the Rockies? And later, at our destination, enjoy a picnic with him in an Aspen meadow while he analyzed whether my boys had a predisposition to high cholesterol based on their medical profile?

Somewhere there are two guys from west Texas who go to a skeet-shooting match every year. On that particular annual flight, they order two drinks apiece for the 50 minutes they are airborne. One is a fertilizer salesman who told me about getting his hand jammed in an airline toilet on a downdraft air pocket.

I collect these stories for what reason? When we fly, we are all raised up off the earth for a time. We may be thrilled or frightened or bored, but we are all out of our earthly milieu for a magical moment of time. Like Rapunzel, we can let our hair down. Whatever is said on this plane stays on this plane.

When I've had a particularly close and meaningful time with a seat partner, I often say upon parting, "Have a nice life." They are usually startled, then break into a grin. Recognizing the ironic finality of my wish, they know their stories are safe with me, well, all except the ones I've told here.

Oh, Oh, Oh For the Longest Time

In the 90s my exercise class danced to Billy Joel's "The Longest Time" released in 1983, a love song about all the things that had happened since he'd been in love, things that hadn't happened for the longest time.

Things are not waiting very long to happen to me anymore. As I get older, I find myself staring at the calendar in disbelief that another month has passed. My older friends report the same. What we thought would be a time of life when days would drag is doing just the opposite. Still, there are moments in the days that have always seemed long—wristwatch-tapping, temporally-hiccuping long.

Time seems to stand still when I'm beating egg whites or cream into mounds of what the recipe encourages as being "stiff and standing on their own." There have been times when I thought my whole adulthood had flitted by while I beat cake batter for four minutes. Ditto for "Stir frequently" on stew pans full of gravy bubbling on the stove. I try to hum an old hymn when caught in one of these stirring vortices.

There is a traffic light near my house that is surely the longest in the city. Neighbors have complained to the traffic department folks about it but they seem indifferent to changing it, especially since there's a disparity in the amount of traffic going each way. Thinking I would write a stiff letter to the powers that be, I decided to collect the specifics. I would be righteously outraged at the ten minutes we had to sit there. But upon investigation, it seems we outliers have to wait a whole two-and-one-half minutes before proceeding. Now I use the time to check my makeup or redial Sirius.

The longest thirty minutes occurs when I'm waiting for the tax preparer to finish the return and tell me how much income tax I still owe.

The longest day is moving day. The longest three days occurs when one is waiting to hear the lab report from the doctor. The longest week of the year is the first week in January, when we're struggling with New Year's resolutions, trying to learn to write the year's date, and ruminating on past holiday parties.

The longest month where I live is August. There's no breeze in August and the temperature soars to three digits. My father used to say,

"August in Texas is no good for anything except to separate July from September."

The longest nine months has always been the human gestation period. I can remember wishing—futilely of course—that I could rest the abdominal beach ball on a table for just a few minutes before taking it up again.

The time between the beach ball's emergence and his leaving home is practically a time warp, and then the longest year descends as the parent contemplates the pitfalls lurking for a freshman in college.

Long nights of insomnia wedge their way into one's life, when the only charm is witnessing the bedside digital clock changing numbers.

And then there are simply dozens of quarky minims throughout one's daily life. There's the time when the plane lands and finally taxies to the gate, the bell dings, passengers spring their seat belts, and then begins the long wait while those ahead start the hara-kiri struggle of bouncing their luggage down on their heads. Meanwhile, back in the terminal, waiting for a loved one to appear after the announcement of the plane's arrival can amount to a century, depending on how enthusiastic the host is about the visitor.

The Roman poet Ovid called time "the devourer of things." Yes, but certain moments of time provide us with tiny stall-outs, tooth pickings, water sippings, napkin refoldings, times when we are truly out of synch with chronology. Frankly, I'm grateful for these stall-outs...they mean a few more minutes of life span.

Student Bloopers

For a number of years, I taught freshman composition and rhetoric at the university level. The course in composition was designed to help them improve their communication in standard written English. At the end of the semester, these struggling, often hapless young people were subjected to the torture of a dreaded Departmental Exam. They had to write a 500-word essay on a subject presented to them only when they stepped into the exam room. The test was designed to see if they could conger up some thoughts on a social issue, organize them, and intelligently discuss them in writing. They were judged on both grammar and content. And a "pass" or "fail" figured heavily in the final averaging of their grade for the course. Those deemed unacceptable by the first reader were further vetted by a second reader.

Out of strict objectivity, we did not grade our own students' papers. They were all turned in to a central place and redistributed to the professors. Because it was the end of the semester, we read hurriedly, without taking time to mark errors or make comments—just a pass or fail.

But when I ran across a particularly unwitting or witty remark, I could not help but copy it down. Priceless! These kids were doing their best, which was only sometimes good enough to be excused from further intense help with the language.

So with apologies to the fine men and women these students have no doubt become, I offer here some of their freshman...well...bloopers, altruisms, double entendres, and just plain beating-around-the-bush, or "I need 25 more words to make it to 500."

One essay question asked them to discuss the differences in large and small families. A student observed that "Parents are a big factor in a family." Especially, "large families are brought about entirely by the parents." Another went on to say that "Many times having a large or small family can be very nice, depending on how the parents go about it." Furthermore, "These types of families [large or small] have a lot in common but are so different. These families range from one corner of the earth to another. They live in the forest; they live in the sea shores; they live in the rocky mountain hilltops." Pretty evident was the fact that

"Generations have gone by and one thing they have passed down to us is the family," and that "Living in a large or small family unit leads to a big step in life." I'll say!

One writer voted for small families: "There are not as many children around to bother them and the children will probably not molest their parents too much anyway."

A student obviously remembering the instructor's admonition to try relating to the reader in a personal way wrote "I leave you, dear reader, with one last thing to say, if you are the oldest in your family you are not alone but if you are one of those younger brats I hope your eyes fall out!" A gentler ending read, "An adult must come down to a child's level and I hope my theme has accomplished that goal." I think it did.

We asked them to write about different kinds of neighborhoods. A sentence which was used to launch the discussion stated, "Two neighborhoods that are from the same town are different." One possible accidentally witty utterance was that "Neighbors are the next best thing to a person." Another focused on crime in neighborhoods: "Many are fighting bad [mad?] at the rise in crimes." One felt she needed a secure neighborhood in order "to sleep knights." To counteract a criminal neighborhood, "...start writing letters to people in high offices, the first being the mayor of my town. If he does not listen or just ignores the letters, my congressman will be the next to suffer." These freshmen already knew the power of language.

There were beginnings that read like preliminary stretches on the driveway before a run: "I, myself, have my own life and attitudes (this, of course, is understood) which propel my tendencies toward areas which I prefer to call a state of mind."

Another began, "Throughout the years, the world has gone through lots of phases in life." Well, everyone has to start somewhere.

When we asked them to write an essay on sexism, they very readily complied. "In the near future," one began, " sex won't have anything to do with how far you go. It will all depend on how well you do it."

"Sex discrimination has also dominated many restaurants. I have heard that some restaurants don't serve black people."

Of course, bigotry got into the sexism picture: "A very peculiar characteristic of a bigot is he is usually going bald."

One writer felt that "sex depended on how temptive her body is." Another deplored sex before marriage, or "premterial sex."

Wondering why on earth they had to write on this subject, a student observed, "I really don't think that there are too many differences because in most cases, it has been understood that the woman should agree with what the man says."

Another sought to inform by definition: "Pornography, in case you didn't know, is the art of taking pictures and writing reading material of and on people while performing sex."

Writing about career choices, a young man who was no doubt counting words wrote, "Some of the careers chosen by students are long, others are short, and some are in between." Unh-hunh.

One career positively shined: "There is a positive side to midwifery and it's not all that bad."

There were many interesting word struggles in the departmentals, in phrases like "the country's ecomony," "he was torchering himself," "it was my interstanding," "she knew she was a lesbeing," and "the boring rountine of life." Reading these "will [and did] enthusiaze the viewer intensely."

It wasn't just freshman comp students who struggled mightily with the English language. In reading the essays of my sophomore literature students, I could see how the talent held, year to year. The second-year mandatory literature classes were filled with inventive, how-do-I-get-out-of-here students. Samples:

"Hawthorne's preoccupation with quilt [guilt] adds sadness to his stories which lead to misery and usually sadistic and moreover fatal conclusions."

"Let's say that if I was going to die under one of the two poets' pens, I would rather die under Wilbur's. It would be more peaceful."

"Camus and Spartre in the contest of this paper..."

"The story is about a boy who thought he was great in everything or at least he thought so."

"This is an initiation story because she was utterly confused and disturbed about herself which caused her several times to end her life."

"It keeps you in the edge of your toes."

Sometimes I would ask them for definitions of literary terms. Their answers were enlightening:

plagiarism: "to bother someone." Well, yes, and what else?

irony: "the tusks of an elephant"; "using very hard words"; "a way of expressing an expression" redundancy: "to have a plentiful supply;" "The smooth continuity of rhythm and rhyme is continual."

dialog: "a conversation between one or more persons;" "a two-sided conservation."

literary romance: "the poetry he says to her in order to make love to her"; "when writings are linked together or have something to do with each other."

I'm feeling a little guilty that I have recounted the bloopers without saying how many things my hundreds of students over the years got right. The truth is, they did, and that is the reason they passed those dreaded freshman and sophomore English classes.

Purses

If there is a hereafter, the first thing I will request is a perfect purse. So far in this life I have yet to find one. Purses are too small, too large or too heavy. They have tacky designs or display hideously large labels of the company that made them. Some yawn widely, inviting entry by unwanted hands, or are snapped or zippered so tightly that each opening becomes a tug of war. Most have dark inside linings and too many or too few inside pockets.

I had one purse that I thought qualified for heaven. It was gray leather, about the size of a large loaf of bread—big enough to hold all my stuff but not clumsy big, with sturdy handles and an easy zipper. It was given to me by one of my sons. I would have it yet but it wore out completely from years of cherished use.

A purse is a woman's most important piece of clothing. It's not an accessory; it's her alter ego. It contains her identity and all the necessities for her life force on the road.

If you're thinking that a purse is not important (and about to stop reading this piece) consider whether you have a backpack. Bingo! Admit it's a purse.

Contrary to what it might seem, men were the first to use purses. Egyptian hieroglyphs show men wearing purses around their waists. A famous purse carrier was Judas Iscariot, whom the gospel of John mentioned "had the bag" filled with gold coins. Ancient literature is rife with allusions to men carrying money in pouches.

Through the centuries, purses took on a bevy of names, dependent on their size, use, and nationality. They were "hamondeys," "tasques," "chaneries," "reticules," "indispensables," and "swete bagges," which were filled with herbs and spices and carried to offset the scarcity of bathing.

The term "handbag" came into use with the invention of trains. A handbag was a smaller version of a lady's trunks stashed in the luggage car. A handbag transported her most personal and immediately needed possessions. In other words, handbags were the first carry-on luggage. Popular designs excessive in buckles, fasteners, locks, and keys are holdovers from the first handbags.

In our border area, a wealthy Mexican man shopping in the Valley can be identified by the prominent black purse he carries. First-world men's fashions of late have been featuring the well-appointed man with a slim briefcase on a shoulder strap. These are purses. I'll bet that, along with important business papers, there's a package of tissues and a stick of lip balm in there, as well as a cell phone, a tin of breath fresheners, and parking meter change.

As the mother of sons, I was subjected to a special burden as they were growing up. When we went somewhere, one would often run to me asserting his right to a boy's carefree existence by asking me to carry an object in my purse that he had acquired. I have lugged home half-eaten sandwiches, comic books, toy cars, and broken watches, as well as Boy Scout manuals and trombone mouthpieces. My husband from time to time would comment negatively on the ubiquitous presence of my purse, and I would have to remind him that my purse was the first aid kit for the family, what with its band-aids, tissues, emery boards, cough drops, and aspirin.

The most famous quote about purses, "You can't make a silk purse from a sow's ear," sends me to wondering if someone, somewhere will one day try to create at least a purse out of sow's ears. It wouldn't surprise me, as they are already made from the remains of hippos, snakes, and cows.

We probably don't take full advantage of purse as a verb, derived, of course, from the noun and meaning to capture or enclose something. There's been a lot of "pursing one's lips" in our recent elections. A more favorable use of purse as a verb means to save, as in to hold on to a valuable item.

If I ever get a perfect purse, I will purse it at all costs.

Jan Seale

Being Gauche and Sinistral

When the rest of the world gets through with their protests, I should like to help mobilize another group—left-handed people. We thousands could march on Washington holding in our left hands signs that say "Left is Lovely," "Left is Deft," and "Go, Gauche!" (the French word for "left").

It takes a certain toughness to get through the world left-handed. As a child, I meekly sympathized with my mother who wrung both of her hands in desperation when she attempted to teach me to knit and crochet left-handed. She ended up sending me down the street to learn the basics from Miss Bessie Clements, a retired school teacher, who had practiced ESP from long years writing on the board with her back to her class, and so could teach me backwards, and often with her eyes closed.

When my first-grade teacher told us to point the tops of our writing papers toward the windows, I was puzzled and positioned mine toward the door. I found a corner seat at the table so I wouldn't bump anybody with my elbow. I moved my milk glass to the left side of my plate. I accepted my piano teacher's judgment that my bass was too loud. I obeyed my father when he asked me not to use his desk pens.

In the early years of my adulthood, I suffered many slings and arrows of left- handedness. Punch ladles had right-handed lips only, causing me to slop punch awkwardly into cups at receptions. Watches could be worn on the right wrist so one wouldn't have to drag leather and metal across a page when writing, but then there were the contortions to wind them, or to see what the date was.

And I wore an angry circular indention at the base of my left thumb from using scissors manufactured exclusively for use with the right hand. Later, when they were available, I invested in a pair of left-handed scissors. But at first I couldn't cut a cat's whisker with them. It seems I had compensated too many years with right-handed ones and couldn't reverse the pull and squeeze to produce the proper tension as the blades closed.

In the days when we frequently wrote personal checks to merchants, many clerks could not resist calling attention to my left-handedness when I was paying the bill with a check. "Look at the southpaw!" they were wont to exclaim to anyone around. Or, "So! You're one of those lefties!" as if I didn't know.

I finally had enough. When I heard one of those exclamations, I would calmly stop my pen, trying for a dramatic location like the middle of the merchant's name, or on the decimal between the dollars and the cents. Rolling Little Orphan Annie eyes, I would say, "Well, of course if you don't want my left-handed check..." Not one of them ever failed to assure me, with lots of nervous laughter, that my check was quite acceptable.

If they continued more subdued heckling, I would fill them in with some presumed diagnosis. "Yes, I'm left-handed because I was brain-damaged at birth."

These days, when I autograph books at signings, the person whose book I am flattered to sign often says, "I didn't know you were left-handed." Maybe it's just something to make conversation. But what's a proper reply to that? "Oh, sorry!" "Now you do." "It's not part of my resume." The one I like is, "Twelve percent of the world's population is left-handed and there are twice as many men as women."

The remark I've never been able to come up with a snappy rebuttal for: "I don't see how you can write with that hand." What I want to say in answer is that since the body is fairly symmetrical, one hand looks pretty much like the other hand, and the same motions which produce right-handed writing can also be used for left-handed writing. To call someone weird and strange, that is, gauche and sinistral, for writing left-handed is about as logical as feeling totally disoriented every time you look in the mirror.

In fact, the only thing different about left-handed writing is that, because our society writes from left to right, the left-handed writer has the disadvantage of obscuring, with the raised knuckles of his left hand, the words he has just written. This is why left-handed people are often noted as writing "back-handed" or "upside down." They only do that so they can see what they've just written, something right-handed people take for granted. Unfortunately, these particular left-handed people are called hookers.

Former President Obama is a famous hooker, seen signing bills with a decidedly curved left arm skirting around the top of the document. This might be a good place to call attention to the fact that an inordinate number of U.S. presidents have been left-handed. Five out of the last six presidents were left-handed, with at least a couple more before that, and the possibility of a number of others earlier, since left-handedness was discouraged for a long time.

The prejudice against left-handed people is not confined to insensitive remarks. Our language is loaded with all sorts of tacky connotations for leftness. In politics, we have left-wingers. In sports, nobody wants to be way out in left field. And who wants to get a left-handed compliment? Or eat leftovers?

In medieval times, lefties were thought to be cousins with the devil as well as less intelligent than right-handers. The Latin word *sinistra* originally meant "left" but took on meanings of "evil" or "unlucky" by the Classical Latin era. The Bible contains more than 100 favorable references to the right hand but 25 unfavorable ones to the left hand. However, one famous passage in the book of Judges notes an elite company of 700 left-handed warriors who could "sling a stone at a hair and not miss."

Aside from waging war with slingshots, are there any advantages at all to being left-handed? Yes. Lefties have it all over righties when it comes to punching in and out at toll gates. Lefties are better at tennis. And they're said to be superior artists, Leonardo di Vinci being our cause célèbre.

Lefties may be more adaptable than non-lefties, what with so many compensations required. They may have a better chance at striking up a conversation at cocktail parties if someone insists on calling attention to the hand they're holding their hors d'oeuvre with.

Einstein, Napoleon, Joan of Arc—I salute you with my left hand. May you never be remembered as gauche or sinistral.

A Hate List

When I was a girl, along with not calling people fools, we were not supposed to say we hated anybody or thing. Oh, we could thoroughly dislike or be annoyed by or disapprove of. But hate was a taboo word in our household. Uttering it was a reason for being sent to one's room to think it over.

Nowadays I rather like the idea of getting to say the word "hate." I even keep a hate list, the way other people might raise violets. My rationale is that by writing down what I hate, I free up some brain space for more pleasant ideas—maybe things I love.

With that guilt-ridden explanation of my hate affair with hate, here are a few things I hate. These are on my ongoing, all-time-hate list. I have hated them for a long time and don't see any remedy for their leaving my life.

I hate a lame noisy grocery cart, one that veers off in a sidewise direction when I'm willing it toward the bananas, or one that clicks along snappily calling attention to me as a person with no discernment when choosing a cart;

I hate stepping on a dog crunchie in the kitchen at 2 a.m. This makes a real, not a virtual, impression on the night prowler's foot, not to mention arousing her fight-or-flight instinct, preventing her sleep for two more hours—her insomnia being the reason in the first place for which she came into the kitchen to get milk;

I hate trying to type "bicycle" or "Egypt" or "bookkeeping";

I hate animals that advertise themselves to be eaten—or rather the ad people who think such a tactic is enticing. "Hi! I'm Porky! My ribs are finger-lickin' good!" or "Gobble, gobble! See ya' Thanksgiving Day!"

I hate for a pedestrian to come to the drive-through bank window after I've already waited through four cars to get there;

I hate folding up maps;

I hate cooking with batter, the kind where you dip the thing once in milk, then in egg, then in flour, and back to egg;

I hate it when the person before me turns the water off in the shower but fails to press down the shower button;

Jan Seale

I hate chocolate cake crumbs;

I hate getting young children into footie pajamas;

I hate clothing labels made with metallic thread;

and finally, I hate mailing tape that rolls back on itself after it's cut, defying the dispenser to make it available for the next use.

Well, I don't plan to give up hating any of these things. What's more, I'll be adding to the list. I hate to think what life would be like if everything was perfect.

Such Stuff as Dreams are Made Of

Lately I have been reading through my dream journals of thirty years, looking for some justification for having kept these accounts of my soul's night wanderings for this long a time.

Early on, I tried to keep my dream accounts without so much as an exclamation point by way of emotional reaction to them. Then a psychic suggested a new way. Now I record the dream as fast as possible—it's a great way for a writer to start the day—then draw two sturdy horizontal lines and write an interpretation. Sometimes I don't think there is one, but as soon as I begin to whine to that effect, the meaning comes slamming down on me. Oh! The road with huge ruts means I'm in a rut...no, two ruts.

If I've had several dreams, I write key words in the margin—tip-offs to remind myself what they were about. Otherwise, I'll get so wrapped up in recording one that the others may fall into that nearby abyss of forgetful-ness.

Reading through the dated journals, I see that the dreams somewhat matched my waking activities. When I was teaching, I spent many frustrating hours at night trying to find the right room in a building, or realizing that I was charged with teaching a certain course and had never shown up for it. Sometimes I'd get to the class and have nothing to say.

During the childbearing years, I often had visions of rocking, cajoling, cooking, and chauffeuring. That was the period where I dreamed repeatedly that I gave birth to a frozen chicken! My grown sons tell me this was not a flattering dream.

Becoming a grandmother of four grandsons, my dreams have often featured little boys. These children need rescuing and protecting. Sometimes they make wise precocious pronouncements. Rather belatedly, and redemptive of the frozen chicken dream, these children are named not their real names but the names of their fathers—my sons.

The loss of relatives and friends precipitates both sad and exhil-arating dreams. I never tell my friends if an ill fate befalls them in my night. On the other hand, I'm eager to share with others if a deceased parent or beloved friend visited me in dreamland, complete with eye contact and voice inflection. These encounters are so very real. They are of the type Alexander Pope commented on when he said, "You eat, in dreams, the custard of the day."

The last few years, conferences and campgrounds dominate my dreams. There are endless workshops, outings, dorms, groups. I travel to these on busses and trains and in cars that often break down on country roads or in sinister valleys. When I finally arrive, I'm bewildered by a huge campus, or the tent is drafty, or it's raining on the campground.

Certain themes have prevailed throughout the thirty years. Buildings seem to fascinate me: I experience vast rooms, staircases, arches, hidey holes, hallways. In their gardens are levels up and down, pathways, ledges. I take comfort in these dreams because they are of the ilk of Jung's famous dream of a house with various rooms, a dream which helped inspire his theory of the collective unconscious in which we draw in our sleep from a cultural storehouse of archetypes.

Church happenings loom large, no doubt because I was brought up in a Baptist parsonage. Parishioners mostly argue and do inappropriate things in the sanctuary.

And then there are the animals. Fish swim in air, peacocks are peevish, parrots attack, and black and white cows and cats wander by.

The lost purse dreams have been the most persistent theme throughout the decades. These dreams include a green straw purse (which I've never owned), as well as my flute and briefcase—basically anything with a strap or handle. My friend Rusty has the lost purse dream too, so I addressed this poem to her:

> Your eyes light up. You have it too.
> Sometimes the one you lose
> is cream-colored, cloth.
> Mine is almost always black.
>
> We agree we have spent valuable
> REM years on fruitless searches.
> The last bad night I had with mine
> was on a bus in Mexico. I looked
> for it among a million chicken cages,
> finally called home without it.

We agree we have wasted
our creative subconscious,
that the dream is 100 percent insecurity,
that we should report to our therapists.
Instead, how about:
if I find your purse in my dream,
I'll return it immediately,
no questions asked?

You do the same,
even if it takes a moving van
and an assistant Scheherazade.

One of the most frustrating things about my dreams is how weak their plots are. When I was a child, I had good strong nightmares, waking up in a sweat and running to my mother for comfort. Chow dogs bit me and robbers jumped out from behind shadowy shrubbery. In my adult years, the predicaments just crawl along, needlings after annoyances after irritations, daring the events to move on decisively and give me a thrill or a shudder. Clothes don't fit, doors don't close, phones ring and cannot be answered. Someone bothered me in a dream recently to say I had not been giving a proper long "e" to "ecological," also that I had not been using "cellulary" properly. I found the need to call a halt to such silliness by waking up.

One person I know enjoys laughing at the visions he has when he is feverish, different from his regular dreams. Coming down with a cold, he dreams math-related dreams, in which a triangle has to be blue, or two crossed masts on a boat must equal the number 4. My favorite dream in the twilight zone of fever is one in which I was driving a mattress down the street.

The importance of plot may have something to do with why starting or ending a modern novel with a dream is verboten. Editors argue that the reader does not appreciate being tricked initially into a false reality. And who among teachers of creative writing has not gnashed her teeth, after wading through an exciting student narrative, to learn "Then I woke up"?

If I look up a symbol, it's usually the wrong meaning for me. Lately, my dreams have red or yellow objects in them. When I noticed the

41

prevalence, that seemed like a good omen—you know, loud happy colors. But when I looked them up in my dream symbol dictionary, red was only blood and violence, and yellow was indecision. So now I'm trying to dream in green. Maybe purple.

"Trying to" is what's called intentional dreaming. Before you go to sleep, you tell yourself you want to dream an answer, or have a splendid new idea, or solve a messy problem. I haven't quite conquered intentional dreaming yet, maybe because I think there's something disloyal about working the deep unconscious that way. I want my dreams to be vacations for my brain.

Lately, I've been wondering what will become of my dream journals when I die. I'm the kind of person who would take a dead relative's journal and read it because, somehow, things like that should be done. I have been reading Uncle Buddy's medical journals off and on for a while now ("took Mary's B.P. at 3 p.m.—185 over 95. Way too high but what's to do?").

A few people make a living studying dreams and I'd gladly give my dream diaries over to these folks if they can prove that they're making some headway on the science. One of their theories is that dreams are scraps of reality the brain is trying to make sense of. Freud thought that dreaming was our way to keep our wishes and desires from waking us up.

Nobody keeps a dream journal for thirty years without some intention. Fuzzy-headed and sleep-drunk, I have persisted. I believe that studying my dreams helps me know that certain someone who is at the heart of my being, that personality on my "committee" that is the authentic me.

And I like the proof that there's more to the world than what we can take in sensorially in the light of day, that there's another world over which we have no control. The workings of our minds and souls are still mysteries. Maybe dreams are the realm of the Divine bursting through the dense fog of our everyday humanity. Dogen, a thirteenth century Japanese Zen monk, thought so: "Who could doubt that a dream is enlightenment, since it is not within the purview of doubt?"

The biggest reason for me to record my dreams may be my sense of play. What better way to begin the day? I like the adventure, happenstance, serendipity, message, even the dark side of dreams, and there seems to be no way to hold on to these except to write them down.

The Clap

Beating our hands together in appreciation for some one or thing before us is an unnatural act. It's not like sneezing or coughing. It is a learned behavior. Babies who are not hooked into patty-caking do not clap. Like a lot of things, no one knows exactly when the habit of "putting our hands together" began. We know the Greeks did, and the Bible mentions clapping nine times. At the end of the plays of the Roman playwright Plautus, there is an instruction for an actor to step forward and say "*Valete et plaudite!*" that is, "Goodbye and now applaud!"

Married many years to a musical conductor, I find it an interesting historical fact that earlier audiences of the modern era were encouraged to clap in the middle of musical renderings—now a definite faux pas. None other than Mozart himself reported that he was so happy that people clapped in the middle of the premiere of one of his compositions that he "went right after the Sinfonie to the Palais Royal—bought [himself] an ice cream, prayed a rosary as [he] had pledged—and went home."

Nowadays, it is considered unsophisticated and rude to clap between sections of a concerto or symphony. If you watch closely in the pause between movements, you will notice the conductor keeps his hands low and busy in front of him—discreetly wiping sweat from his brow or turning the page of his musical score. When he wants the audience to clap, he will turn around and invite them with a flourish and bow to acknowledge the players by beating their hands together.

My husband would occasionally call clapping into play for an entirely different purpose. When he made a preliminary visit to a concert hall to determine suitability for performing there, he immediately tested the acoustics by clapping his hands together and listening for reverberation, doing this over and over from different locations in the hall.

A famous modern-day incident of clapping occurred at the 1937 conference of the Communist Party in the Soviet Union. The ruthless Joseph Stalin finished his speech and delegates rose for obligatory applauding. Then they found themselves caught in an awful dilemma. Who would quit clapping first? They looked around at each other helplessly as they considered the consequences of being the first to break it off. As the writer Aleksandr Solzhenitsyn reported in *The Gulag Archipelago*, a hapless director of a paper factory gave up, quit clapping, and sat down. Immediately the whole hall followed grateful suit. But the brave man's actions were not without consequence. That night he was arrested on a trumped-up charge and went to prison for ten years. Stalin's henchmen had been watching.

Now, if sound technicians in that Moscow hall nearly a century ago had had the benefit of Youtube, they could have hooked up the currently available "Applause Sound Effects For 12 Hours" and all gone home to supper, leaving the vicious tyrant to bask all alone in the sounds of enthusiastic applause. And the paper factory director would have been the happiest.

Researchers claim that clapping stimulates blood circulation and that receptors in the hands connecting to sensory fields in the brain increase brain activity. Clapping may also engage the body's healing responses. Vanna White must be the healthiest ever for her thirty-two years of clapping for, mind you, *big block letters* on "Wheel of Fortune."

Intentional clapping, for example, done in musical games or with singing, is said to cause children to have neater handwriting, do better in composition, and make fewer spelling mistakes than their non-clapping classmates.

As children, we were brought up to observe certain mores in clapping that seem to have gone out the window today. Time was, you did not clap for yourself. And you did not clap for any of your family being lauded by others. You sat or stood there looking happy and grateful. At present-day occasions, politicians clap wildly for each other, for their clapping audiences, and for themselves. The recent presidential election revealed a variety of styles: Candidate Clinton's precise prim forward clapping and Trump's hefty waist-level ho-hos, all the while avoiding his swinging open coat. First Lady Michelle excelled in fast long-fingered motions and her husband in careful dignified Presidential approbation.

If you think about it, clapping for ourselves and each other, for music that touches us, dramas that succeed; applause for our children as they walk across the stage for their diplomas; for service men and women deplaning from tours of duty; for politicians having plowed through speeches bravely beleaguered or cheered—all these gestures are signs that we are still living, breathing, moving our limbs, demonstrating bodily that we have some kind of visceral reaction to what we are experiencing. Watching television does not usually find us on our feet applauding, shouting "Bravo!" and turning to our neighbors for agreements of delight (well, except for football).

We should probably be glad for this deeply ingrained public sign of approval that we practice with little thought or restriction. If you think about it, what could possibly be handier?

Sayings I've Got to Quit Saying

"Tighter than Dick's hatband." "Happy as a dead pig in the sunshine." "The mules see the barn." Right off, after my title, I'm not sure I want to quit saying these things. They come into my speech via my Southern ancestry and seem natural with my predisposition for metaphors. And they remind me of my parents, whose mouths they floated from over the supper table, in doorways, in backyards, and on auto trips.

In our sped-up world of words, where today's cool is tomorrow's passé, I get some funny looks when these expressions come out of my mouth. In an effort to legitimize them, I have researched a few. "Tighter than Dick's hatband" has a number of cloudy origins. Dick might be Richard Cromwell, son of Oliver Cromwell. Dick was apparently incapable of serving as the Second Lord Protector, thus his tight crown. I use it to mean stingier, the key word being "tighter."

Happily, "Happy as a dead pig in the sunshine," (which some people wince over after I've reported that as my state of being), is a seemingly clear referent to the actual look on the face of a dead pig who's been left in the sun awhile. Its flesh shrinks and the lips draw back in a smile. Cute, huh?

"The mules see the barn" comes straight from my father's childhood in Arkansas. After a day of plowing with a team of mules, the father and sons would start home—hot, dirty, tired. When the mules rounded the bend and caught sight of the barn, they went to their happy place, stepping up their pace, snorting, and generally showing mule glee. It's a very useful term, meaning that a consequence will be inevitable given the facts.

Cotton is the natural subject for a Southerner's speech. To "chop cotton" is to stay with a job, especially an unpleasant one. Actually, cotton choppers do not chop cotton. Rather, they hoe the weeds around the cotton plants. "Tall cotton" comes from antebellum days. If you were lucky, you might have a crop of tall cotton, plants that have matured to tall stalks with fuller blooms easier to pick. Occasionally, you could find yourself in tall cotton, where an atmosphere of riches and high living prevailed.

My mother was apt to "chew cotton" or "spit cotton." These disdain-ful conditions occurred in her mouth when she was very thirsty and hinting for a Dr. Pepper. I sometimes have that malady myself, with the appropriate fix in mind.

Mother had a unique call to a meal. She yelled, "Suppertime! All ain't here better hide over." I'm ashamed to admit that, as a girl, I never thought to ask her what that meant. For that matter, I heard it as, "Allain't here, better hightover." Only a few years ago, I asked her about it and she very practically explained that in the game of Hide-and-Seek, if you haven't been discovered by the "It" after a certain time, you are probably not going to be and they might find you days later, curled up in the coal chute dead as a doornail. (See? I can't help talking in metaphors.) Sooo, if you haven't made it safely to "home," or if you haven't been successfully tagged by "It," you should hide over, that is, hide someplace else so you can be more easily discovered and thus not die in your very clever hiding spot and miss supper altogether.

Poets are often deemed impractical and I certainly fit that category. I despair easily if I can't locate a needed object. I'm always asking a nearby person to help me find what I'm searching for, only to have him or her say, "It's right here." My standard reply is, "If it'd been a snake, it would've bitten me." This seems to let me off the hook for appearing stupid, pleasantly distracting the helper until I can take my found belonging and exit.

Pigs, mules, snakes. Southern speech is full of animals. Commodities may be "scarce as hen's teeth," a man "drunk as a biled owl," a child fleeing its bath "naked as a jaybird," and a downtrodden person "rode hard and put up wet," a very unhealthy treatment of a horse. The origin of "how the cow ate the cabbage" is apocryphal; seems cows would have difficulty biting into a head of cabbage because they have no front teeth, and, even if they did, cabbage would flummox them with serious gas because of their various stomachs. Who can say how this all translates to mean telling someone off? The message is usually an unpleasant truth and has the sting of rebuke. You may have to tell someone how the cow ate the cabbage if you "can't trust him any farther than you can throw a stick." And you may have no more time to bless him out than "two shakes of a lamb's tail."

Things connoting motion seem to have a linguistic life of their own in Southern speech. There's "fast as greased lightning" and "going like a house afire." But sometimes a man may have "a hitch in his git-along" or even be moving as slow as "death warmed over."

Along with seeking therapy for Southern metaphors peppering my speech, I probably should stay on for a few sessions to bring me up to date on certain terms. It is hard for me to say "beauty salon" when in my heart it is a beauty shop or beauty parlor. My backyard fish pond has no fish in it so why do I keep calling it that rather than a water feature? Condos and townhouses tend to be lumped into apartments in my brain. The glove compartment in cars is now a glove box, all except in my car. And my stock broker has asked me to call him a financial adviser.

There are surely better things to do than mope over my regional dialect. Okay, I think I'll just go get busy with my rat killing. Either that or frying bacon. Please don't judge my linguistic abilities by this essay. Don't hold it against me if I decide I can't get rid of this Southern speechifying. If you do, I'll be madder'n a wet hen.

Filling in the Blanks

I don't know about you but it seems on this far side of life I have spent an awful lot of time up until now struggling not to do nothing. It may be that my brain won't let me be as peaceful as my mind tells me I should learn to be. You know, meditate…calmly sit with palms up… gently lead the mind back to nothingness. I once was told by a person operating a crystal on a chain behind my head that it was swinging like crazy, getting the energy from my head, as in manically. Maybe that's why it could be medicinal for me to write down ways to distract my dizzy busy brain.

As a preacher's kid, I spent hundreds of hours in church. Hopefully, some were focused and spiritual. But many could have been boring except for some applications of sanity. In another essay in this book, I've told about the game of hymns we played as teenagers in church. Here are some of the things I learned to do long before that to keep from going crazy in prayer meeting and yet not call attention to myself. God forgive me!

Sucked in my stomach 20 times. Rested. Did 20 more.
Tried to think of five syllable words.
Made an appraisal of all scar tissue on my hands and arms, including
picking at pre-scar tissue, aka scabs.
Took my bracelet and ring off. Put them on. Took them off.
Deep breathed to the count of eight—four inhaling, four exhaling.
Pushed the cuticles back on all ten fingers.
Tested the automatic cut-offs of the veins in my wrists by damming them with one finger while tracing along their lines with another.
Did tongue exercises.

But that was then, this is now. Everywhere I go, in doctors' waiting rooms, at airports, in the post office line, I find myself outnumbered and outclassed by people busy on their cell phones and other devices. Some are texting; others are playing games. Very few are reading articles on nuclear energy. How do I know? If they're nearby, I unashamedly look at their

49

screens. I have a cell phone too but it's in my purse. I do not multi-task well, and besides, I seem not to have as many friends as these people do. So what do I do while all this tsunami of communication is taking place?

If I'm in the doctor's office, I whip through all the golf and business magazines first. Then, if I haven't been called (and I usually haven't been), I make a study of the shoe wear in the room, trying to decide what kind of personality lies north of the feet. It's a little like nineteenth-century phrenology where cranial features were thought to indicate character.

If I'm waiting to catch a plane, I have plenty of entertainment listening to the conversations of people on cell phones, with absolutely no compunction about actively listening as these people complain about their hemorrhoids, sing songs to their lover in a foreign tongue (I am not kidding), bawl out an employee, or give a recipe for banana bread. Me? In addition to eavesdropping, I while away the time clutching my boarding pass and wondering if I should go to the bathroom one more time.

Worrying is a good way to spend time when one is trapped. Some time back, in a long security check line at the world's largest airport in Atlanta, I worried about whether the mint leaves and high-protein powder in my carryon would be conceived as marijuana and cocaine. They weren't, but on a recent trip little sculptures of seals wrapped as gifts for my grandsons (Get it? Seals) had to be unwrapped and examined by TSA because the x-ray saw them as "lumps." On the return leg, I was carrying the product of my grandson's money-making band project, cinnamon muffin mix. This box had to be wanded as a potential explosive. These adventures keep me from having too much time on my hands as well as feeling inferior to people who have more cell phone friends.

The post office queue in my area is very, very interesting. There are winter Texans in breezy shorts and tennies having their mail stopped or started. There are people mailing money home to Mexico. There are frantic people in the wrong line trying to get their passports renewed. It seems very few are actually just buying stamps. While I'm waiting, I spend time trying to remember what kinds of commemorative stamps I have determined via the internet that I want. Yes, I'm the one who comes to the counter and asks to see the album displaying the various stamps they have in stock. This last time I got Superwoman, the planets, and the reenactment of the Stamp Act riot of 1765. These were worth any amount of time standing in line though I'm sure others in line were bored while I looked through the book.

Waiting in line at the grocery check-out, I make up stories based on what I see in the baskets ahead of me. One lady has pickles, mayo, and cat food—cat food salad. This one has a bouquet, a chocolate cake, and peanuts —office birthday. Here are eight gallons of orange drink, ten packages of vanilla wafers, a big bag of Dum-Dums--It's party time at Head Start.

As a detail person, I can always find something to occupy my mind. It must stem from my almost two-year stint in bed as a child with tuberculosis. With no TV or electronic toys, I learned to keep myself from going crazy by inventing stuff to do in the hours, days, weeks. When I made my way to the foot of the bed under the covers, I was a squirrel. When I pressed and held my fists against my eyes, I could see colors and floating shapes. I invented an action game by coughing my TB cough at the edge of one side of the bed and then trying to hold the next cough until I speed-rolled to the opposite side. I traced the lighted dial of the Philco over and over with a fingertip. And I pretended I was living in a tent city by poking my knees, feet, and hands into various configurations under the covers and seeing how long I could sustain the positions—a kind of one-sided Slinging Statue game.

The nerve and verve it took to keep from getting bored as a six-year-old locked in bed with TB and not very sick has come in handy to combat mind-numbing boredom in my adult life. "Going to my happy place" at the beginning of an MRI has new meaning when they tell me to lie perfectly still, then trundle me into that steel cylinder for the longest twenty minutes of my life. I don't care if they do let me pick out the kind of music I want to listen to and instruct me to squeeze the little hand-held bulb if I want to summon them. I have to fight down the panic, telling myself that I am still agile enough to wiggle out if World War Three comes while I'm being zapped.

I'm a member of a reading group of like-minded women who meet once a week. We started as a meditation group, morphed to meditating ten minutes at the first, and now we take a vote on whether we want to meditate at all, the choice usually depending on whether our dedicated leader is there. I am secretly happy that we now have non-meditation choice, because I have never been able to still my mind and think of nothing for any prolonged time, like ten minutes, especially surrounded by friends I've been dying to talk to since last week's meeting.

My friend Peggy told me that she'd figured out insomnia was God's way of getting our attention, that is, having us lie there and, as simple as it may sound, just *think thoughts*. She's probably right. I've lain there many nights thinking about it.

A favorite line of mine by Robert Lewis Stevenson expresses my sentiments, "The world is so full of a number of things, I'm sure we should all be as happy as kings." It's a little sappy for our day and age, but hey, Robert, I'm willing to keep looking for a number of things, that is, the details, the smorgasbord of natural and unnatural life laid out at every turn. Sure beats the blahs.

My Navel, My Self

I have lost the ability to perform omphaloskepsis. That is, I will never be able to contemplate my navel again. Without my foreknowledge or permission, it was removed.

"My navel's gone!" I said rather too loud, peering at the long bright pink incision traveling across my waist. Close on that initial discovery, I had the most curious thought: Will I have to surrender my birth certificate? And, to whom?

It's just that no one told me beforehand that my navel was going in the trash. So I am left to belatedly appreciate it. I'm not mad, just "weirded out," as the kids say. I didn't know until it was too late that our navels are vital organs, the Skin Bowls played on our birthdays, our bodies' Good Housekeeping Seals of Approval.

I discovered my navel's absence about noon of the day after the surgeon had practiced his art by removing a lot of my insides and patching up a hernia. Enough a'ready.

The assistant surgeon came in and ripped off the color-coordinated pink vinyl bandage. For a few minutes, I remained smitten with his neat sewing skills and heard from his very own lips that yes indeed, the operation was a success. Then the doctor smiled, pulled the sheet over his artwork, and left.

But something kept nudging my consciousness. I raised the sheet and looked again. I hunted left and right, up and down. I wondered if my morphine dispenser had malfunctioned and I was in some special delusional state. My navel was nowhere around.

I'd been requested in pre-op to sign off on various organ locations, literally initialing them in black marker. But no similar request had been made of me about my navel.

To be sure, I'd asked the surgeon earlier if he could do a tummy tuck while he was surgically visiting that region. He frowned. "An abdomino-plasty? We'll have to have a plastic surgeon standing by for that. It may take another week to get a consult with him." I was 2,000 miles from home and he'd just told me I had a 40% chance of cancer. Twenty seconds and I had my priorities straight; let's move ahead—fast. I sighed, guessing I'd have that same Venus belly when I woke up.

But I didn't. I had a tight flat belly, gratis, from the surgeon or his assistant. The report read that "grossly unremarkable skin and subcutaneous tissue *including umbilicus*" had been removed.

Mine was an innie. It didn't ask for much, maybe a little drying after a bath. But now that I can only dream it, I'm remembering that it was good for a reassuring pat. When this happened, there were internal radiating lines extending out like a sunburst. There was a Zen-ness to it. Any time we want a little break from the tedium of a committee meeting, there it is, an innocently placed erogenous zone waiting to give reassurance that yes, we *have* been born.

Now too late, the Tantrikas warn me I have no center. My solar plexus chakra is not only out of balance, it's like, not even there. "The navel is the place where the body receives, transforms, and stores external energy and forces. Thus it needs to be free of congestion and tension." Mine is free all right.

There are over 500,000 navel sites on the Internet. ("Did you mean to search for *naval* entries?" Google inquires helpfully.) Among other things which I learn now, now that it's too late, is that belly dancing is very good for one's health. Also, I might have become famous as a collector of navel lint, putting it in jars, and exhibiting it up and down the World Wide Highway (I am not making this up!—the guy with this website must be napping with a flock of sheep). If I had a navel, I could invest in an array of navel jewelry: rings, belly knockers, tapers, spikes, and barbells.

Or I could have my picture taken lifting my blouse demurely for the street photographer in Brussels, and listed beside my navel's portrait would be a real cheap trans-Atlantic phone number.

If I had a navel, I could cure my arthritis by keeping two sesame seeds snug in it overnight. And if I happened to be a vampire, you could effectively kill me by driving a stake through my heart *or my navel*.

In short, if I still had a navel, I would have a throne for the Creator Herself, from which She would direct all my functions.

At the softball game last week, I got to talking to my friend Shirley whom I hadn't seen in a while. She'd had a tummy tuck too, only she'd had the full-price one, not like my two-fer. They'd made her a new navel. "Want to see it?"

We headed for the women's room. Shirley raised her shirt. There it was, pretty little tucked omphalos of a thing, just as innie as could be.

"How did they *do* that?" I wailed, bitter with navel envy. Furthermore, my friend appeared to be centered, balanced, and was radiating energy. Shirley was Exhibit A for a wholeness retreat.

Now it was my turn. I showed her my unsmiling grim zipper of scar.

"Oops," was all she could manage. Then, trying for some soothing sister talk, Shirley said, "But doesn't the real one itch sometimes? Don't you just want to scratch it good?" I felt consoled. Despite Shirley's pretty arti-ficial navel, she and I could suffer phantom navel together. And I realized that even if I had a new navel, built to order like Shirley's, it would never replace my loyal old one.

When the aliens abduct me, they're going to be shocked to find that I'm a cousin of theirs.

Sweet Milk and Light Bread

Two terms that chime in my childhood ear are "sweet milk" and "light bread," neither of which are in most dictionaries anymore. They are good ole Southern terms.

I once observed the famous Southern poet James Dickey ordering a meal in deep South Texas...

"And what will you drink?" asked the bilingual waiter.

"I want swa-et mee-ulk," Dickey answered.

The waiter looked to the rest of us for translation. It took a while but we Southerners with agrarian backgrounds finally got across to the recent immigrant from Mexico that the honoree of the dinner simply wanted milk, that is—*leche.*

Later, I took a poll of my older adult students. To some, sweet milk was whole milk before the cream was removed. To others, it was the opposite of buttermilk.

And light bread? One man was adamant that it was any quick bread like biscuits. Others said no—it was sliced white bread.

Light bread brought to mind the Light Crust Dough Boys of the 30s, a country band formed to advertise a flour mill. The band went around Texas playing and singing for gubernatorial candidate W. Lee O'Daniel on a flatbed truck drawn up on courthouse lawns. But their songs were all about biscuits, not true light bread.

W. Lee O'Daniel has the distinction of being the only man ever to defeat Lyndon Johnson in a political race. In Texas, tasty biscuits could very well have done the trick.

The internet says that the term "light bread" does not mean either biscuits or white bread. Light bread is leavened bread, sometimes called "loaf bread," as opposed to heavy bread, or, to Southerners, cornbread. I don't care what the official Google reference is, "light bread" was always, but always *white* sliced bread.

We children preferred light bread so we could see our teeth marks in it, or roll it into balls before popping it into our mouths to feel that peculiar reaction of saliva on starch. I recently was seated in an Italian restaurant so near the accordionist that I began to feel I might go deaf before the evening was over. A diner nearby suggested I roll a bit of bread into a ball and use it as an ear plug. Voilá! "Edelweiss" in an echo chamber.

Ask any group of teenagers what sweet milk and light bread are and their blank faces will tell you that these double terms laden with such nostalgia for our old supper tables are anachronisms. The milk today is 2 percent, or 1 percent, and the bread is whole grain or wheatberry or extra thin-sliced.

Communing over food was hugely popular in Bible times. Jesus' ministry was so often centered around food that it's hard to find a passage that doesn't mention a feast, or sustenance, or a thirst honored. There were banquets and bread broken, drinks from the well, suppings, gatherings around the table, picnics of 5,000, and cloistered upper room private dinners.

Eating together is an intimate act. Think about it: we open a hole in our faces, we put in animal or vegetable matter, we pour juice on it to soften it, and after a while performing a motion with our faces like a washing machine, we roll the mass back into our gullets and with a slight grimace and a bulging of the neck, we squeeze it downward. Pretty personal, eh?

We've learned to do this with perfect strangers at airport standup counters, and seated back to back, or side by side with total unknowns in restaurants.

Will we always have two-term food items? Now we order ice tea (not "iced tea") or bottled water, specifying with or without lemon or lime, and with little or much ice.

"Chicken-fried chicken" seems a little over the top to me, as does whole-fried turkey at Thanksgiving. (Really, it happens.)

Does food taste better if it has a double name? Like "hot dogs" or "roast beef"? Like "tuna fish" or "blackened salmon"? Like "pan pizza" or "hot wings"?

Then there's the cross-breeding of perfectly good food, such as "turkey jerky" or "chicken fajitas" or "tuna lasagne." It may be that the purposes are multiple—to achieve greater variety, make certain foods more palatable to the finicky, use up excess, or just be clever with a dish of delectable words. Whatever, this phenomenon only seems to build. We'll be concocting unlikely go-togethers for years to come.

Maybe "sweet milk" and "light bread" tasted so good because their names were definite, specific, unequivocal. In other words, all sweetness and light.

II. Admonitions

A Thump on the Head

There they sat, cross-legged on the floor, twenty-five third graders with upturned faces, name tags hung around their necks, eager for the first of several weekly visits by the poet. My plan for the day was to talk a few minutes about what poems were, then to recite one or two to tickle eight-year-old fancies, and end up by leading them to write a class poem together.

But a minute into my opening, a boy on the first row named Alphonso raised his hand. He was small and grimy. "Miss!" he called urgently. "Look! Look at my head!" He held up the hair on his forehead and showed me a yellow and purple goose egg. It appeared to this three-son mother to be about four days old. "Will I be all right?"

I glanced at the teacher. She smiled and nodded. "Oh, I think so, Alphonso," I said breezily and went on.

But Alphonso was still worried. Maybe this lady wasn't being honest. He interrupted again. "Wait, Miss! Do you think they are going to operate me?"

A boy named Juan next to him decided to help him out a little. Juan turned to Alphonso and said, "Look, Miss! I can push it in and out."

I gave a little gasp, murmured another assurance and tried to go on.

Alphonso persisted. He waved his hand wildly in the air. "Miss! Listen, Miss! Do you think I'm going to die?"

I was dumbfounded at his anguish. Maybe Alphonso had received all kinds of assurances from his family and teachers, but somehow, they hadn't been enough. He needed the word of a total stranger, as if I would bring evidence from another world that the bruise was not fatal. He was suffering deep distress.

I would have to wing it. Into my mind popped the poster-size Sunday School artist rendering of Jesus beckoning the children to come to him. "But Jesus said, 'Let the children come to me. Don't stop them! For the Kingdom of Heaven belongs to such as these.'" (Matthew 19:14 NLT)

They tell us everything we have ever seen and learned is stored somewhere in our beings. At this moment I was glad for any resource that

61

would come forward from my past.

    I reached out and beckoned Alphonso to come stand beside me. He scampered up. I put one arm around him and smelled his schoolboy playground sweat. "Stand close," I whispered. Then I placed my other hand gently over the bump, and said, "I solemnly promise you, Alphonso, that when I come back next week, you will be well."

    Alphonso sighed deeply and shivered, then returned to his place.

    And this time, I got the chance to move forward with my master plan.

    When I think back on that day, I know that what I did was terribly ordinary, a little risky, and frankly, expeditious. Alphonso was surely going to get well, whether I said so or not.

    What I remember are the important lessons that I myself learned:

    A child's hurting assumes precedence over other plans.

    Comfort is a grand priority in this world.

    A little love is the antidote.

    The kingdom of heaven is made up of small hurting Alphonsos.

Touchdown

The big muscles needed for labor in the past have been reduced to those in the fingers as we click, tap, punch, swipe, and snap our way through our gadgets. We are a multi-generation of touch handlers.

As children, we now-older folks were taught to be gentle with machines, to move the dial on the radio slowly and smoothly. We were to be cautious as we wound our watches, stopping before we over-wound them and ruined them forever. When television came in, we were sent to the screen to change the channel with care, pausing the knob to look back at our parents, checking on their reaction to the program being shown.

My father had very broad fingers that would have made it virtually impossible for him to dial a rotary phone. But the end of his index finger on his right hand was conveniently scored with a circular scar that reduced the tip of that digit to a narrower version, allowing him that one finger for dialing. That was all he needed. When his grandchildren asked him how he got that strangely shaped finger, he first told them that God had given it to him as a special dispensation for dialing a phone. This elevated the rotary dial phone to a beatific gadget. Then he told them the truth.

When he was a small lad in a one-room schoolhouse in Arkansas, the older children convinced little Hollis to hold the neck of the hand water pump during recess so they could pump their water for drinking. The two parts, pump handle and connecting pipe, had worked loose. As he held the connection, the top part of the heavy pump slipped up and came down on his finger, effectively cutting off the tip.

With blood everywhere, and sobered classmates, he ran home with the beheaded finger, where his mother poured kerosene in the wound, recapped it, and wrapped it in a rag. The flesh of the tip eventually reconnected with the rest of the finger, giving him, later on in life, a convenient smaller dialing digit.

By the time my children started button-pushing in earnest, there were hardier gadgets and more of them to operate. One teenager learned songs on his guitar by listening to professional tapes until he could execute the passages. I can still hear the clicks of his tape recorder; he was a lightning-fast wonder at play-pause-reverse-play.

Another of them became a camera bug, entailing complicated settings and executions of swift commands, all while the subject might be more than likely moving away. He was the one who said wisely as a toddler, "We don't push people; we push buttons."

A third child became a French horn player, with a complicated trio of actions between his valve-pushing fingertips, his breath, and his lips.

One would think we had reached the ultimate in tiny buttons on our gadgets, but of course, if you've been thinking ahead, you know that there's another iteration of commands, that being the screen stroke. Now our button-pushing is limited to typing on keyboards, everything else being touches, strokes, and swipes.

Next, our eyes become button-pushers, as delicate sensors pick up our blinks and eye directions. And our voices give commands to our friend Siri on our cell phones. Vision and sound replace the delicate sensitivity of our fingertips. It's a bit of a shame, in that our fingertips possess such marvelous traits as being able to distinguish temperatures and textures. They do neither when they push buttons, but they make up for it by responding to pressure, with pounds per inch and depth of pushing.

One button that has not diminished in size is the one that starts my car. Foot on the brake, I enjoy the power trip that ample sized button produces.

Button-pushing is really all about power. The symbol being used universally now for on/off on our electrical devices shows an incomplete circle with a line hanging down through it. The line stands for "on" and the circle for "off." To make things more interesting, there is a *hard* power button and its *soft* counterpart, with an audible click of the former and a mysterious nothing for the latter.

It's hard to underestimate the control over our lives that the voluntary use of our senses exerts, whether it's button-pushing, touching, or blinking. Already, we have to be careful how we stroke our laptop touchpads, lest they send us off to unwanted destinations in the cyberworld. And we're told by communications researchers not to gaze too hard at another person unless we intend to activate with our eyes a specific line of communication with them. Did we need experts to tell us this? There's a phrase in a saying, "pushed my buttons" that will one day be outmoded. In the future, the irritated person will declare that the offender "touched my screen" or "monkeyed with my blinks."

Change

Recently I was studying a family photo taken when there were lots of teenage cousins in picnic clothes standing side by side, smiling broadly, barely able to keep from giving finger horns to the one beside them. Their parents, my only sibling Nan and her husband Edward, plus my husband Carl and I, stood as healthy forty-somethings managing to be the parents of teenagers with what looks like energy and humor. Completing the picture were the matriarch and patriarch, our mother and father, a little stooped, a little wan, but game for the picture and loving the occasion.

It struck me how death had edited the photo. All the adult men are gone, as well as the matriarch and one granddaughter. If we re-took the photo today, whoever's left would have to stand closer together.

Someone said the only person who likes change is a wet baby. But there it is, in all its unpredictable swift uncompromising nature. If you think about it, the only thing we can know in this life that will be inevitable is change. Change will happen. Change is always there. Sometimes we make it happen, and that's okay. Sometimes change forces itself upon us—not so good.

When I teach memoir writing workshops, I ask class members to think of a change in their lives, an important change. It could be intentional or unintentional, anything from losing a loved one to buying a new car. Then, they try to list three things they lost and three things they gained by such a change.

For example, suppose the change is something our Winter Texans are going to do by going north. They might list under "losses" Tex-Mex food, being with other Winter Texans, and square dancing. Under "gained," a Winter Texan might say that the change from the Valley to their permanent home up north means being with their grown children and grandchildren as well as reuniting with their church, clubs, and lifetime friends. That sort of subject is easy enough to show losses and gains.

But an unintentional change presents a different picture. In the case of the death of a parent, the losses are easy enough to name. The child might list wise counsel, grandparents for his children, and a hero or heroine to look up to. The gains are much harder to list, but with some thought, students come up with them. The parent's death gives them a reason to contemplate the mysteries of eternity; it may make them determined to do or say meaningful important things; and it may give them a greater sense of self as an adult. We've all experienced the wonderful gatherings of large families when an important member dies. And, if the truth is known, for some adult children, they admit that the loss of a parent who has had a lot of needs means they have much more time for their own interests and family.

In every loss, there are gains—some we certainly would not want or claim, but they're there. We experience a mix of feelings, sometimes in close proximity—regret and relief, fear and courage, uncertainty and discovery.

The early American author, Washington Irving—who gave us "The Legend of Sleepy Hollow" with its feckless Icabod Crane—also gave us a pithy example of the relativity of change: "There is a certain relief in change, even though it be from bad to worse; as I have found in traveling in a stagecoach, that it is often a comfort to shift one's position, and be bruised in a new place."

A news story featured a man who had become a paraplegic who set for himself a goal of ascending several thousand feet up a frozen waterfall in Colorado. He made it, after a fierce struggle of eight hours. He said later of his disability, "Life is not over when there's a disability; life just begins again in a new way." Change. Life beginning again in a new way.

Joseph Campbell, the great mythologist, said, "Sometimes we have to give up the life we had planned in order to live the life that is waiting for us."

When painful change occurs, change that we did not choose, we can be assured that we will not necessarily be happier or more fortunate, but we will for certain be deeper in spirit. We will have the benefit of a fuller range of feelings than those who seem to have lived unsurprising superior lucky lives.

We might "be bruised in a new place." I would not make the case for intentional bruising, but at least we know we are alive by the display of blood vessels in that place. We changeling humans have the famed theoretical physicist Stephen Hawking on our side, who has observed, "Intelligence is the ability to adapt to change."

Resting (if not standing) on the Promises

In the Fifties and Sixties, there was a game teenagers played in church to keep themselves occupied. We would take the hymnal, go to the index, point out a title, and add the phrase "between the sheets" to enjoy the resulting sense. Thus, "There's a Sweet, Sweet Spirit"—between the sheets. "Sleepers Awake!"—between the sheets. "What Shall I Give Thee?"—between the sheets. You get the idea. Try it next time you are trapped with a hymnal.

Another game was to sing loudly into the ears of our surrounding friends certain new lyrics to the hymns we were supposed to be intoning, such as substituting "The Constipated Cross-eyed Bear" for "The Consecrated Cross I'd Bear" and "Bringing in the Cheese" for "Bringing in the Sheaves."

The names of the songwriters could offer a salve to the boredom of a seemingly endless church service. I liked trying to pronounce silently Ithamar Conkey and Lizzie S. Tourjée although Ballington Booth and Haldor Lillenas could also entertain me. Alexcenah Thomas and Edward Plumptre provided a moment or two of study. But what was P.P. Bliss thinking when he didn't sign his hymn compositions with his full given names, Philip Paul, using instead those suggestive initials?

My fascination with hymns sometimes takes up more space in my brain than I have reserves to allow. Poke me in my sleep, give me the first line of "Just As I Am" and I can sing all six verses by heart. I was raised in the Baptist faith and the Broadman Hymnal put its dark green stamp on me.

Many of the favorite mainstream Protestant hymns were written in the 19th and early 20th centuries. They are full of metaphorical pictures of labor, with titles like "Work for the Night is Coming", "Rescue the Perishing," and "One More Day's Work for Jesus." I spent summers with my aunt and uncle out in the Panhandle of Texas and if I listen hard, I think I can still hear those wheat farmers at the Gem Community Church as they sing, "We'll work 'til Jesus comes...and we'll be carried home," with the lowest voices chiming "We'll work" as an echo in the chorus.

Other hymns cheerfully belie the prospect of finality in death, such

67

as "When We All Get to Heaven," "Bound for the Promised Land," and "Sweet By and By."

Certain favorite themes pop up through the hymns. Conquest hymns are popular: "Hold the Fort," "Am I a Soldier of the Cross" and "Onward, Christian Soldiers." So are storms: "From Every Stormy Wind" and water of all sorts, from Jordan flowing "Deep and Wide," to "Jesus Savior, Pilot Me" and Jesus being led "Down to the Sacred Wave." Crowns, gardens, rocks, stories, time passing—these are elaborated frequently. Of course, the all-time winner is the cross, with "The Old Rugged Cross" in some circles right up there in popularity with "Amazing Grace."

Speaking of which, the popularity of "Amazing Grace" astounds me. It is estimated to be performed ten million times a year worldwide. Agnostics in football stadiums swing and sway to it when blues entertainers offer their stylized versions. Do they understand the words, that they are "wretches," lost and blind, saved by something called "grace" that they would be hard-put to define? By the way, much has been made of the fact that a converted slaver, John Newton, wrote the words to this beloved hymn. Less known are the facts that he owned slaves some six years after he saw the light, and that he only wrote "Amazing Grace" some 25 years later.

The gospel hymns are rife with wretches, demons, and blood. Not infrequently are there perfectly abominable words and badly mixed metaphors. Take for example, "There is a fountain filled with blood/ drawn from Emmanuel's veins/ and sinners plunged beneath that flood lose all their guilty stains." Don't try to visualize that. Wikipedia observes, "This is one of the first hymns William Cowper wrote after his first attack of temporary madness."

For a number of years, my friend Karol and I delighted in sitting at the piano, playing and singing the hymns we cut our teeth on. Karol was raised in the American Baptist tradition in Iowa, and I in the Southern Baptist in Texas but we find a great commonality in the hymns we knew from childhood. When this songfest started, my husband, a classical musician, would quickly vacate the premises, as we howled in delight at torturing him.

Karol and I dote on special passages in the hymns and can hardly keep them out of our correspondence. Through the years, one in particular has been useful, from the hymn titled "Come, Thou Fount of Every Blessing." The second verse begins, "Here I raise mine Ebenezer," the reference being to the prophet Samuel building a stone monument to celebrate God's help in victory over the Philistines. Karol and I raise our Ebenezers—sometimes in glee, on other occasions in protest. We may reference others whom we note have raised their Ebenezers in our presence.

Feeling an uneasy peace with the gospel hymns, I decided to use some of their titles as launching places for poems about faith. These came to be a section in my book *Nape*. So I have poems titled "On Jordan's Stormy Banks"—this one a narrative about my father seeing a turtle in the creek as he was immersed in baptism; another called "Pilgrim, Pilgrim, Why Do You Tarry?" about how the objects all around us beg to be taken care of, to be worked on; and "My Faith Looks Up to Thee" which has the speaker able to see the throat pouch of a remarkable singing mockingbird on a wire.

Much has been made of the last scene in the movie *Places in the Heart* with Sally Field and Danny Glover. After turmoil in the community, the characters come together to take communion in the local church while the choir sings "In the Garden." Maybe it's because I'm from Waxahachie—where the movie was filmed—that I am so struck by the use of this gospel song by Charles Miles published in 1912. I went to school with a couple of the extras singing in the choir, and the preacher was our insurance man.

In the soundtrack of the movie, the hymn sounds exactly like I heard it 65 years ago in the First Baptist Church in Waxahachie. My father would occasionally sing solos in church, with my mother accompanying him on the piano. One of his favorites was "In the Garden." I hear him singing, "And He walks with me, and He talks with me, and He tells me I am His own."

Not to ruin our soft fuzzy feeling for "Amazing Grace," let me quickly add that these old gospel songs have great power over us—and if we respond to them by recoiling from their outmoded lyrics, the peppy over-verbalized stanzas and their whining repetitive choruses, we also take great comfort in them.

For some, it is that aching loveliness of their child-self long ago in a brush arbor revival, past their bedtime, swatting mosquitoes and looking forward to that churned ice cream that awaited them after the final stanza of the invitation hymn.

For others, it is the summons to memories of their parents and grandparents rousing a chorus beside them as they keep time with their

69

hymnals, punching the air gently before them.

And of course, there are those early-day hymns that have genuinely lovely words and melodies. All but the most calloused nonbelievers may succumb to the charm of "Abide With Me" and "Day in Dying in the West."

For some, there is a phrase that catches in the throat upon hearing or singing these oldies but goodies. I can remember a time in church when I was entertaining my two-year-old grandson Luca. We stood to sing and I hoisted him into my arms, not daring to leave him unguarded beside me in the pew. At the sound of the organ's introduction, he paused his busy self and rested his head against me. The song was "Blessed Assurance" and I can still recall the sensation of extraordinary peace realizing that, whatever the words meant, here was my blessed assurance—of generativity, of ongoing-ness.

The old gospel hymns may speak to us of our present state of grace but they may more often take us to a place in memory and circumstance that brings us up short, to a place completely outside our rational, scientific, tech-oriented world. They are, in the end, a good thing to rest our promises on.

I rest my case.

Troubles Go Double on the Road

So you're finding it hard to interest anyone in your vacation stories? Forget the awesome colors of the Grand Canyon. Skip your reaction to the Sistine Chapel. Just concentrate on accounts that involve double troubles.

Remember the time the bear climbed on your hood in Yellowstone? Now that by itself made you laugh nervously. But if you keep thinking, you'll remember that was the time your camera was in the trunk.

A freeway can be a frightening thing when you're in an unfamiliar part of the nation. But wasn't the cloverleaf in Chicago where Bobby upchucked? Face it: That sort of thing isn't going to happen on Farm-to-Market 121 outside Dimebox, Texas.

Our car never gives trouble—except on long bridges, or in Mexico. In big cities, it makes a habit of getting us lost—always in the riot districts.

Once we camped at a place in Louisiana where there were so many mosquitoes we wanted to leave at 3:30 a.m. But we didn't have enough gas to drive to an open gas station.

You don't ask a dog if he can wait 17 more miles until you get to Puducah for a rest stop. If your dog is kin to ours, he needs to go *now*—adjacent the 33,000-bird turkey farm you're passing.

Another good combination is a rainstorm and an attack of diarrhea. The timing on these things boggles the mind. Once we made our own incredible journey across Idaho in the only rainfall they'd had that year—after purchasing and eating a big basket of cherries in Utah.

There's a certain sense of appropriateness about a twosome like the navigator getting the map folded up just as the family approaches the crucial all-points intersection.

Or the only driver breaking his right ankle on the skiing trip to Colorado.

Then there's that endearing duo we all remember: You've jiggled the crabby baby for 200 miles. Finally, he dozes. But it's noontime and the others are hungry. Time to stop, and wake up the baby.

Our most stunning double-or-nothing, though, was a child's nosebleed—in the East Room of the White House.

A Woman's Worth

In the "Writing Your Life Story" courses I have taught over the years, older women have often shown near amnesia for the lives they've lived. Men forthrightly volunteer, "I was a radiologist for 30 years" or "I am an electrical engineer." They name themselves. They have identities.

Women are apt to stammer out something about raising six children, being married twice, maybe teaching school or being a secretary. They have *done* things; they just haven't *been* anybody.

My own take on this difference is that women have traditionally held so many different jobs, at once or in quick succession, that the tasks, and more importantly, the dignity of those tasks, blur in women's psyches, like all the colors put together becoming gray.

I am not excluded from this definition. I have clerked in a dry-goods store, been a deputy tax collector, a secretary, a flute and piano teacher, taught junior high, high school, and college English and creative writing, mothered three sons, and made a home for a husband. Somewhere in there I managed to write books.

Women's role as family-preserver is dizzyingly diverse, fraught with interruptions, emergencies, contingencies, children changing constantly, schedules, food, cleaning, illness, transportation, feelings and celebrations. In effect, women as caregivers live everyone else's life as well as (and some-times instead of) their own.

I don't mean to discount the role stay-at-home fathers have taken on in recent years, nor their care-giving, nor the number of jobs any one man might have held. Yet, statistically, women in this country are still over-whelmingly the main caregivers of both their children and older members of the family who need care.

So does it count if you've worked at a couple of dozen different jobs in your life? Yes. And is that bad? No. The only thing bad is to believe, in a curious way, that your life has been nothing because it has been so much, and that the things you have done—birthing, rocking, stirring, driving, folding, cleaning, cooking, consoling, cajoling, doctoring, listening, admonishing, finding, volunteering, sponsoring—are not worth remembering and taking seriously.

In Lillian Schlissel's collection *Women's Diaries of the Westward Journey,* there is an astonishing lack of detail about childbirth along the migration routes. A tacit silence prevails about an event that surely formed the apex of joy or sorrow for women on the trail. Often the only way the reader knows of newborns is in the report of their short life, after the mother was "taken ill." We can only conclude that the diarists, along with Victorian modesty, were mindful the world would not be interested in these "women things."

In my writing classes, I have to remind older women of how they held the schools together with PTA, the churches together teaching Sunday school, the families together providing supper for years on end. Women need to see that their patience, hope, discipline, intuition, love, and constancy of daily labor had worth, even if these things were so multifarious and mingled that they cannot be labeled with a single name, that what they did as ordinary was really the most extraordinary, because it kept the world going.

Women need to celebrate their lives. Because they are worth it.

Lewis Carroll, unwittingly perhaps, wrote a scene for a girl in *Alice in Wonderland:*

"Who are you?" said the Caterpillar.

...Alice replied, rather shyly, "I-I hardly know, sir, just at present—at least I know who I was when I got up this morning, but I think I must have been changed several times since then."

Let's hear it for the chameleon life. For the patchwork quilt life. For the life of variety. The put-together life has strength in its glue.

Jan Seale

There's Been An Accident

It was 1964 on a Saturday morning in May. I had baked a pie and was frying chicken when the phone rang. The voice tried to sound calm but the news it brought stunned me. My husband's brother, Larry, a young man of eighteen, was unconscious as a result of a freakish swimming accident on a senior high group outing at Padre Island forty miles away. Would I tell my husband and have him tell his parents?

The next hour was a nightmarish jumble—trying to find my husband in town, racing to his parents' home only to discover they had heard the news and were driving to a town between ours and the beach where we had learned Larry was being taken to a hospital.

When we got there, the doctor came out of the emergency room and told us Larry was dead. I remember his saying distractedly, "Don't ask me how in God's providence such a thing can be!"

We stood silent in disbelief. Time stalled in midair. We were incredu-lous.

Back at the home of my parents-in-law, we participated in the numbness with the many details that suddenly confronted us. There were relatives to notify, funeral arrangements to make, friends to receive. In retrospect, I don't remember ever letting myself cry that day.

After all, I asked silently, who am I to grieve openly? I was just a sister-in-law to him. I could at least bolster up my husband and his parents. They had lost so much more than I. Besides, I had two small children to care for, and one was old enough to be struggling to comprehend what had happened. I felt I had to be composed.

So I acted almost automatically. We got the sleeping pills for his parents. We went to the cleaners with the sad task of getting the boy's fresh-pressed suit. We quietly put away the graduation gifts that had started to come in.

After the funeral, I spent several tiresome but busy days writing thank-you notes, meeting guests and spending time with the older relatives who had come. Then one morning I awoke with nothing left to do. I had run out of all the barricades between me and grief. It struck me with great force: Larry was gone; our world would have to do without him.

Perhaps I could have accepted his death more easily if some of the circumstances had been different. But he had been the brother in my life since I had never had one in my own family. I had helped him with his homework; we had many long talks. He babysat and gardened for us. When he was fourteen, he spent six weeks with us in the summer while we were still in college. It was a wonderful time—the exchange of love and fun that passed among the three of us.

Maybe I could have tolerated the tragedy better if he had been a so-called "ordinary" teenager. Because he was so unusual, I'll never know. Mature always beyond his age, he was president of his senior class and would have graduated as valedictorian in a few more days. He had recently been named one of our state's best high school musicians. He had a music scholarship waiting for him at a top university.

His personal attributes were as attractive as his formal honors. He was thoughtful of his parents, loyal to his church, kind with children, funny. Quiet but not shy, his tall, slender being was an asset to any group he chose to join.

And so, with the circumstances as they were, I became more and more bitter about his death. When everyone else in the family seemed to be feeling better, I grew worse. I cried during the day while my husband was at work. He had started to smile again and play with the children in the evenings and I didn't want to prolong his mourning by telling him how I really felt.

Each night when I tried to sleep, I asked myself over and over why Larry had to die. Why couldn't it have been someone old with a full life behind them? Why was this young person who was such an asset to the world taken away from everything he enjoyed so much? I couldn't even begin to accept his death.

Sometimes I would wake in the night and my mind would torture me with all the events of that awful day. I would break out in a sweat when I thought of how the boy must have felt when he lost consciousness in the strong undertow. This idea so haunted me that I woke my husband one night to talk about it. He admitted that he too had nightmares about the fear that must have filled the boy. The conversation proved to be a relief to both of us but it didn't stop my emotional erosion.

As the days wore on, I thought less about the details of the tragedy and more about the implications. Why couldn't a similarly tragic accident happen again, this time to one of my own sons? I began to see potential harm in everything they did. I worried when they climbed a tree in the yard. My heart beat fast when they were away from me, even out of my sight. All the children's accidents I had ever heard of paraded through my mind. I worried incessantly.

And coupled with all my anxiety for them was a feeling that whatever I did to try to help them grow up really didn't make any difference at all. I had always wanted to be a good mother, to see that their needs were well-met. Now I found myself wondering why I had bothered. What good did it do for us as parents to plan and hope for them? They might be taken away just as Larry was.

This boy had been nurtured carefully by his parents with the hope that he would have a fulfilled and useful life. What difference had it made? I couldn't see that any of their careful work with him, their struggling, their pride, their unselfishness had been of any value.

I was further mystified by their attitude. The day of his death, his dad said, "We can be thankful he had all the pleasures of being young without any of the hardships of being old." They never asked for pity as the time went by. They did everything they could to keep from being a burden to anyone. They went to new eating places, planned a vacation, re-decorated a room. It became more and more incredible to me that they could go on—apparently accepting his death as part of some divine plan.

I seemed to lose more of my faith instead of regaining it. You tried to do the right things concerning your children. You made the decisions carefully. You played games with them. You were careful that their inocula-tions were current, that they took their vitamins, that they went to the dentist. And after all that, maybe, just maybe, they would get a chance to grow into happy, worthwhile adults. But the odds seemed so great against them.

I began to think of my children as useless, sweet but useless. I wondered how each thing we did related to their future. Did it matter that I read to them each night, that I explained about caterpillars turning into butterflies, that I explored the ground with them for new rocks? If life was going to treat them exactly as it pleased, whatever I might do seemed wasted.

Any joy I had when I was with them disappeared. "Mommie, are you having fun with us?" my four year old asked anxiously one day when he saw I really wasn't *there* while watching them play.

I quit insisting that they brush their teeth at bedtime. What was the use? I even begrudged the struggle I had to get their high-top corrective shoes on their feet. And washing their faces became a stupid ritual I was performing just for the sake of my reputation as a mother.

Every moment of my day came to be tinged with bitterness. I was a total pessimist. I because opposed, at least silently, to anything constructive, to any phase of living that needed hope to make it a success. And I felt ashamed and guilty that I had given up.

I know now that with each day, I was closer to needing professional help. But I didn't try to get it. I didn't even tell my husband about my feelings. Each day was more miserable than the one before.

One day I visited our doctor for treatment of a sore throat. He seemed to sense I had something else bothering me, for after he had prescribed medicine for my throat, he asked how I felt about Larry's death since some time had passed. I found myself telling him everything—the depres-sion, the bitterness, the resignation. It didn't take him long to analyze my state of mind. This veteran of the Holocaust shook his head decisively, took my hand and said with his deep Jewish accent, "You can't give up. That is very wrong of you. Life is a precious commodity."

He went on. "It would be a terrible thing to ruin several lives because one was shortened. Since you have been forced to do without him, you cannot afford to carry this event in your memory to a place where it hurts everyone around you."

As he talked, it dawned on me how futile it was to premise my life and those of our children on one tragic event. I had generalized my grief beyond all reason. My doctor never knew how he changed me that day, how the fact that he sensed something was wrong and talked to me on a mere hunch cleared my muddled mind and spirit.

But I walked out of his office with far more than a prescription for a sore throat. He had given me the tonic for beginning again. I resolved on the way home to *try*, even if it was an act at first.

It was hard. I had regressions. I still had some tears, some nightmares. But I changed. When I caught myself slipping into the old forms of anxiety and depression, I thought of Brutus's reply upon hearing that his wife Portia was dead in Shakespeare's *Julius Caesar*. Grieved but wise, Brutus sighed, "Well, to our work alive." The jobs I could not do with faith yet, I simply did automatically. "To our work alive," I said to myself.

Perhaps the thing that helped most during this period was time itself. It may be a cliché but it is also a powerful truth: time is a great healer. I found that nothing—not anything I read or thought or did or said—helped like the passing of time. Not any consolation made as much difference as the months and years that followed.

I came to see that Larry's life, which I had been counting as a total loss, had not been a loss at all. We had gained so much from his time on earth. He had shown us that being a teenager and being irresponsible were not synonymous. He had been an example of goodness to dozens of his friends. He had brought eighteen years of delight to his parents, his brothers and sister. After many months, I caught myself saying rather comfortably, "Do you remember how Larry laughed?" or "He planted these flowers, didn't he?"

But the way back to a truce with fate was not always smooth. One day, struggling with my old sense of fatalism, it occurred to me that the young man who was gone would have loathed what I had let his death do to me. I went back to a copy of his valedictory speech, which he finished a little while before he went swimming that day. He had written:

To be aware of our problems is necessary, and I am not saying that we should cease to be aware of them, but to be so involved with them and to place such an emphasis on them so that we become depressed, is to inject disease in our spirits that can be fatal.

I'm sure I had read his speech over in the days following his death. And I had heard it read by a classmate at his funeral. But now I listened to it in the light of my own healing.

And finally, more than once, I drew on the faith of the boy's parents to renew mine. They cared for *our* children. They never solicited sympathy. They accepted gratefully any small pleasure that came their way. They expressed genuine interest in the new college life of Larry's friends.

It was an experience I do not wish for anyone else. Yet I know there are many others who struggle with grief the way I did. My grief was not the grief of wise people who build their sorrow like a giant snow sculpture, and then, finished with their activity, welcome the sunshine that will dissolve the structure. My grief was rather a tiny snowball, held at first in check by my careful hands and later, as it broke away from my grasp, becoming larger and larger as it rolled down the mountainside of my life.

In the end, I welcomed reality, not the reality that says everything is going to turn out all right or that nothing could ever happen to my children. It is the awareness that where our children's lives are concerned, we are dealing with a miracle—not a sure thing in our finite concept of time and space. I felt myself reaffirming the goodness of life, whatever amount of time we are placed on this earth. I accepted my children's lives as a beautiful bonus to my own, meant for enjoyment and celebration. To shortchange the quality of life because we know we are mortal strikes me as the ultimate in ingratitude.

A few years passed, and my husband and I were entrusted with another precious son. As the child grew, the resemblance of him to his late Uncle Larry was truly remarkable.

We can say with Saint Julian of Norwich, that at the end of time, "Thou shalt see thyself that all manner of thing shall be well." And of adversity, "in falling and rising we are ever preciously kept in one love."

Through the Eye of a Needle

One day when I sat down at the sewing machine to mend, I found I could not thread the needle. Oh, I was *in* the moment, all right: my hand was steady, and I could see the tip of the thread and the hole in the needle. But when I painstakingly started the thread tip through the eye, I was surprised, over and over, to be just a hair's breadth off. I had gotten older.

My mother used a needle threader but I'd never paid attention to the process. It was one of those things that grown children like to ignore as being quaint and irrelevant in their own lives. Only after the old folks depart do these things blindside us.

A threader looks like the filament of an incandescent light bulb, with a little foil tab at the base to grasp it. Now I hunted through my sewing drawer and located a small tin, once a lozenge holder, labeled "Mother's last sewing kit."

At this point my eyes glistened. In her prime, my mother had been an expert seamstress, so much so that my sister and I had very few store-bought outfits before we went off to college.

Opening the box, I found a rusty safety pin, a tiny set of pliers, a screw driver for eye glasses, a thimble, two paper clips, a seam ripper, and the blade of a butter knife. No thread or needle in this "last sewing kit," but, lucky for me, there in the bottom lay the prized threader.

It took me a while to figure out how to use it. Put the end of the thread through the flexible wire triangle, poke the extended corner of the triangle through the eye of the needle, draw the loop of thread to the far side of the needle, making sure the end of the thread is safely past the eye, and withdraw the threader. It is a sneak play.

Jesus used the threading of a needle in an extravagant metaphor. "It is harder for a rich man to enter the kingdom of heaven than for a camel to pass through the eye of a needle."

Many have found this observation bewildering and incongruous with Jesus' other teachings about fairness. I am bewildered but not threatened by it because I will never be either rich or a man. Did Jesus say this to frighten rich people? To encourage camel contortionists? To get rid of the rich young ruler dogging him on the road?

Beats me.

Theologians have been arguing for centuries about this passage. It seems so biased, so unfair. Some thrash through the ancient language to insist that "camel" translates "cable." Or that "needle" is really a small gate in a city wall. Others insist Jesus was speaking literally: it *is not* possible for a huge beast to squeeze through a sewing implement. They conclude that Jesus made this raw pronouncement to counter the then-common Jewish belief that a man who was rich was obviously virtuous.

A little later, and perhaps seeing the shocked expressions of his listeners, Jesus mollifies his story: "Humanly speaking, it is impossible. But with God, everything is possible."

So, we find it doesn't say there'll be no entering heaven for the financially enhanced. It's possible, just hard, hard, hard.

Maybe they'll have to kill off their camel. Maybe they need to look through their mother's last sewing kit. Maybe they'll have to make up a last money kit, fill it with irrelevant items, and leave it as an object lesson for their children.

Small metal objects in cough drop boxes. Mismatched items. Mislabelled by careless sons or daughters.

Let's say the big Pfaff professional sewing machines are going to have a hard time. They've worked at good deeds all their lives—turned out garments, sewed curtains, embroidered towels. But if they can't be threaded, woe unto them.

Only the threader in the bottom of a cough drop tin...a serendipity out of our control...some tiny way out...a humble legacy. Will that be the way that matters?

The Downside of Downsizing

The downsizing movement has been going on for some years, not negligibly unaided by "Hoarders" on TV. Like you, I tell my friends I never watch that worthless addictive show but the truth is, I pause on it for long intervals when I'm surfing. I'm there just long enough to utter remonstrances: "Gross!" "Sick!" "Sad!" during commercials. Most of us are not willing to sleep on top of our Christmas decorations and old pizza boxes. We dislike cat poop aroma. We'd rather not walk room to room on a carpet of trash, our heads touching the ceiling.

Some of my acquaintances among older folks—no doubt addicted like me to watching "Hoarders"—have gone to extremes not to be hoarders. They have thrown out decades of collecting. They take photos of photos, then load the antique shops with vintage pictures of their relatives. If you don't believe it, just look at all the unidentified, charmingly-framed, serious but goofy-looking characters from the nineteenth century that stare down at you as you dine at Cracker Barrel.

My friends' main rationale is that they don't want their children to have to deal with their stuff when they're gone. Their clean-out usually coincides with their decision to give up their house and go live in an apartment near their children in some big city halfway across the United States. A survey of friends who have done this has been very enlightening.

One friend was moved by her daughter and son-in-law from a charming woodsy setting to a stark ranch-style in a city with no trees. Then the daughter and her family moved to Germany. So my friend moved to the mountains to be near another daughter. This daughter is too busy for her. Ditto another friend who moved to the city to be near her grandchildren. Not only does she not get to see her growing grandchildren but she's been instructed by her busy daughter, who found her the apartment three miles away, not to call unless she's "fallen and can't get up."

I don't know all the circumstances of these strains between parents and their grown children but they send a red flag to those who might envision a cozy relationship with their grown children in a setting where they try to start over at what's supposed to be a revered age, sometimes without transportation, and with no accessible friends, clubs, churches or neighbors.

Another variation of downsizing is that practiced by a good family friend who has since gone on. In his seventies and widowed, he felt he should minimize his holdings since he planned to travel extensively, so he asked his children and their families to come one weekend for a grand haul-away. He ended up with a TV tray, two vinyl lawn chairs, a hot plate, and a Styrofoam ice chest. A little embarrassed by the helpfulness of his children in denuding his place, he made it well enough for a short while, that is until he met a sprightly widow eager to join him and have fun. When they married, he got to go shopping for all new furniture and appliances to replace the things his children now owned and enjoyed.

Some years ago I read a book on downsizing. Grant you, it was a very small book with a plain cover—the author had no doubt downsized her information. One curt instruction that I did not follow was to buy all your clothes in black and gray. That way you could dress without thinking about whether things matched, saving time. I am too pale and drab to want to save that much time. I need aquas, cerises, chartreuses.

To me, one painful result of my friends' downsizing is to see the books I've authored being sold in the secondhand shops online. But, you ask, How do I know they are my friends who are getting rid of my books, not just some stranger who accidentally bought the book in a weak moment one rainy Saturday afternoon? Because in describing the book ("in good condi-tion with no markings") these cyber-store owners often give the inscription ("to Mary Lou, my BGF forever") and then "the author's name," which they've already given in the general description. When I see this, obviously Mary Lou's top-flight status in my roll call of friends needs altering. If you are reading this and consider yourself one of my best friends, pullease rip out the inscription page before you sell my book online. That way, you can continue to be my BGF.

I recently had a fit of discomposure that left me contemplating a move from the house I have occupied for 42 years. My yard needed too much work. My house was like its owner, still livable but not getting any younger, somewhat okay but needing more and more maintenance to keep it that way. An attractive townhouse was available and I began to visualize a change, one that would permit me to downsize like I thought I should be doing anyway.

I took a trip, preoccupied with the possibility of such a move, but when I came home and opened the front door of my vintage house, a wave of pleasure went through me that I was home, home, home. Later, a friend pointed out that I could downsize my things without having to move out of my house. I could throw away and give away and sell right down to the bare walls in the house where I was. I came to understand that downsizing and moving, although they often happened at the same time, were not automatic go-togethers.

My in-town son helped tip the scales, for now. He said, "Mom, you've done a pretty good job of keeping up anyway. So now, if you have a choice between getting everything ready for us to take over when you're gone, just go have fun. We can take care of your stuff later."

Keepsakes. Look at the word. Things to keep for the sake of _____. I believe in those. I have my mother's wedding hat, my father's French beret. I have recipe cards in my mother's handwriting, manuscripts of sermons my father typed with two fingers. To give these away is not downsizing. They are one-of-a-kind, voices from my grandchildren's ancestry, explanations of their roots, their quirkiness or honesty or predisposition toward certain things. I hope they will keep them, treasure them, look at them once in a while.

Old bills. Tax return copies. Icky mugs from travels. Clothes too small or large. Art projects never finished. Uncomfortable chairs. These can all go, the sooner the better. I absolutely refuse to be the subject of a "Hoarders" documentary.

The Possibility of Greatness

Everything written about New York City must needs be positioned in the pre- or post- of Nine Eleven. So it was in the simple pre- of 1998 that our grown son and his father and I went for a few days to the Big Apple. The most that we heard of American English during our stay was at the Broadway plays and musicals. Swirling around us—in hotel elevators, on the streets, in museums—was a predominance of German and French, with Spanish, Italian, and Japanese close behind. The Deutsche mark and the lira seemed to be holding up very well. From those who helped us in the delis and cabs we think we heard Farsi and Hindustani and Mandarin and Haitian Creole.

On a glorious Sunday morning we took a cab down to Battery Park and clamored aboard a ferry for the requisite trip out to the Statue of Liberty and Ellis Island. A couple of hundred of us were aboard, including a group of frisky French young people not only making but acting out animal sounds near where we sat on the upper deck.

I was trying to think of how to say, *"S'il vous plait*, stand on your own feet, not mine," when we drew near Liberty Island. France's gift to America became an awesome presence. We forgot all about the French pig and goat mimicries. They did too.

No long-range viewfinder from atop the Empire State Building prepares one for the immensity of Our Lady of Liberty. There she stands, a huge verdigris goddess bidding the huddled masses come and breathe free.

Her eyes focus somewhere past the Verrazano-Narrows Bridge, on out into the Atlantic. Her torch-bearing arm is not tired. Her diadem does not give her a headache. She seems undisturbed by the thousands scrutinizing her.

A number of us sprang unexpected eye leaks at the familiar symbol. I can see how her serenity, the calmness echoed in the tranquil folds of her robes, would be a beckoning spirit. If I came newly across the Atlantic and under her shadow, I would feel welcomed to this land.

A little later, walking the halls of the beautifully restored Main Building of the Ellis Island immigration center, we studied a chart showing the swell of 12 million immigrants through those doors in the first half of this century, the decline of immigration at all entry points during the wars, and the resurgence beginning in the 1980s.

Then, for a while, I wandered off from son and husband who were studying a display that interested both. After a bit, I keenly realized a thing I had been only dimly aware of in the preceding days of sightseeing: I could pick out the voice of our adult son anywhere in a noisy, crowded space.

All the while I thought I had been giving full attention to the displays, I had been tethered to him and his father by his voice as they walked about talking. The mother-child bond had been minding the store, thank you, decades after its beginning.

Absently staring at the displays, I began actually testing out what I had just discovered. A young Hispanic woman called to her husband across the Great Entry Hall, *¡Traemelo!* and the man brought the toddler to his mother.

It was one of those rare moments when one's understanding clears and the puzzle pieces fit. My mind flipped back to a diorama we'd seen the day before in the Museum of Natural History. In an imagined first family depiction, a skinny womanoid with a babyoid shoos away a jackal while a hairy manoid pokes at an antelope carcass.

The human family is still the basic unit. Nations are just families of families. From the Central Europeans, vacant-eyed from their weary weeks at sea in 1904, to the malnourished sunburnt Mexican woman whose entry point was "Beeville, Texas 1918," to me, a visitor from South Texas standing there in the late 1990s, warmed by the thought of primordial bonding with kin. We are all connected in our significance and our insignificance.

There has been a recent call in our country for us to re-examine our suspicions of each other, our long-held prejudices and wrong-headed views of differentness. At long last, it's occurred to us that America's unique contribution to the history of nations may be our ability to live together in strength and harmony as a multicultural society.

We all need to feel properly humbled by our smallness and our transience on this planet, by our little tourist boats and our fleeting Sunday mornings. Yet we need to be able to move about in the crowded room of earth and still pick up the voice of our individual family, our uniqueness.

Now, more than any other time in history, there is a giant torch-bearing ideal that challenges us to evolve into a nobler species. Tolerance and civility. Compromise. Dropping prejudice. Learning from each other. Enjoying rather than fearing this canvas of cultures. Grateful to be one of its colors.

We have precious few alternatives on our crowded planet. Freedom is an equal-opportunity employer. It beckons us to accept it, with the corollary that we grant it to those around us as well.

We are, truly, all in the family.

Listening Up

Are we all talking so much we don't know what we're saying anymore?

The other day a well-meaning person told me to "Have a nice day and pass it on." It sounded just fine when he said it, but then I began to think about the possibility: Would I want a nice *used* day from anyone else? I decided I couldn't do that to another person—pass on a secondhand day, no matter how nice it was.

Lately I've been listening to myself more and what I'm hearing isn't as interesting as I had once imagined.

I'm sure there were times when I bored my husband. He sat through many accounts of weird things that happened in the grocery store—like the time I noticed when I got to the car that the $7 lipstick I thought I'd bought was lying wanly in its little plastic tray in the bottom of my grocery cart. Neither I, nor the checker, nor the bagger had noticed it hadn't gotten paid for.

The wind was blowing. It was their fault. I needed to get home. But my late father took this moment to speak up: Right is right and wrong is wrong. It's not yours. Go pay for it.

So I trudged back into the store, found the clerk and made a valiant effort to get her to let me pay for it without having to stand in a long line.

At this point in the tale, I paused, half-expecting my husband to congratulate me on my honesty, but he was sound asleep.

Then there was the time recently when I found myself being scintillating on the subject of contrarian dishwashers. Twice, mind you, twice—I told my dinner guests—I had gone to the appliance store nearby with the intent of buying a new dishwasher. Mine had gone to pot overnight. The glasses murked, the plates crudded, the silverware dulled, the Teflon utensils grayed.

The first time, the salesman suggested I get a plumber to look at it. Our famous Cuban plumber said, "What you want of me? It just fine. Maybe you use less soap?"

So I crippled along, trying different combinations of buttons, sometimes "Light Wash/Heated Dry" or "Pots and Pans/Air Dry." Finally, it got so bad I swear the dishes looked worse after they were washed than when I loaded them in.

(Are you still with me?)

The second time I went to the appliance store I begged the man to sell me a dishwasher, but he said he didn't have the color to match my stove and refrigerator, and besides, all I probably needed was a product which he sold but was out of at the moment, something called "Dishwasher Magic." But I could go to the supplier's and get it. So I went across town to the supplier but they were also out of it and it wouldn't be in until the next Tuesday.

(At this point I notice people are making a ceremony of buttering another roll, or slowly rotating the ice in their well-washed glasses.)

I can recall two friends—well, actually three—who have uniquely registered their boredom in my presence. As I am about to deliver the punch line of a story, one begins to hum softly, sometimes "Brahm's Lullaby," sometimes "The Way We Were."

Another begins yoga exercises, suddenly intent on The Swan and one time even doing Down Dog as I sat on her couch with my legs crossed sipping a glass of wine, thinking we were having a nice ladies' chat.

The third friend does something I've adapted for my own boredom level when I can't listen anymore on the phone. She asks if she can call me back in a little while. This works well for heartbroken friends from whom you've heard it all before.

My grandchildren's no-spank parents have a strange but somewhat effective technique for disciplining their pack of little boys. If the kiddies are given a command and do the opposite, they are reminded, "You are not *listening*." If they perform handily, "*Good* listening!"

Lucky for me in my dotage: they're being trained in the importance of listening, and might automatically pay attention to *me*, foggy-headed and rambling, when they come to visit.

My friend Sally the therapist is proud of the rage she goes into if a client tells her he is bored. She has demonstrated this to me: "If you are bored, it's your own damned fault! Don't ever, ever say again in my office that you are bored! I won't stand for it!" I have been careful not to be bored around Sally.

A line in the "Desiderata" by Max Ehrmann counsels, "Listen to others/ even to the dull and the ignorant;/ they too have their story."

The real question is whether to admit boredom or to say you are never bored.

So here's the bottom line: Be kind to me when I'm boring, and try not to bore others more than necessary. And if you find yourself being bored, be inventive: think of some way to get a little take-home out of the situation.

Oh, my dishwasher…I know you want to know: Well, the problem proved to be that the dish soap manufacturer had taken the phosphorus out of the formula, and in our area, with its hard water, that proved disastrous. The solution is to add a cup of vinegar to every load.

See there? Useful information out of a really boooring subject. (Eye roll here)

Little-known Facts for Campers

How about a few tips on the art of camping, based on a cross-country trip we took one summer to Washington, D.C.?

The first suggestion is that you *not* take any kind of tent or overhead protection. Cots, sleeping bags, and a blanket or two will do. Camping is partaking of nature, and there's nothing like a light shower at 2 a.m. to make you one with the universe. If you can't manage that, settle for waking at dawn blanketed in Virginia mountain dew or Alabama sauna. Wring out those bedrolls at dawn. You'll find the dampness stays in nicely all day as you travel to the next place.

Another important tip: Buy your child a new pair of tennis shoes and then try, the first night out, for a campground with a camp dog. When you register, just inquire whether the proprietor has a large friendly dog who likes to visit around. If so, put your money on the counter. When bedtime comes, have your child put his tennis shoes in a prominent location, some place like the foot of his cot, or the seat of the picnic table.

Dogs like a little fun, and the camp dog won't be able to snitch them in the proper spirit if your child leaves his shoes on the ground beside him. Next morning, rouse the whole family to fan out over the acreage to look for the shoes. If you're lucky enough to get a wide-ranging camp dog, your possibilities for sustaining the hunt until noon are excellent.

Be sure to choose your location carefully in a campground. Look around for campers who seem to be Doing Their Thing, or who are likely to Do Their Thing Later. Heads up for large tubs of iced-down beer, people humming songs about sleeping bags behind couches in Phoenix, resting their heads on other persons' stomachs. Pull in right beside these free souls.

But if you stubbornly refuse to give your children a valuable social experience, then by all means go to the most remote area of the camp. It will usually be in a gully and this is a perfect way to show your children the nation's inland waterways. A fifteen-minute downpour will reveal your barbeque grill afloat, with your pre-schooler in it. Your kids will learn the mysteries of the earth as they watch your loaded station wagon sink lower and lower into the red mud. They'll be excited by the violent wind as you struggle to tie down your tarpaulin.

Don't stay in a campground that's too wild and undeveloped. Try to choose a place that's been humanized. Watch for parks with lots of regulatory signage:

NO YAWNING
TWO BATHING CAPS REQUIRED IN POOL
NO STREAKING OF ONE YEAR OLDS
NO BATHROOM TRIPS AFTER 8 P.M.

Camping is so cheap that you'll probably have a jolt, as we did, when you get home and figure expenses. We found that it cost more to kennel our dog in our hometown than it did for the five of us to sleep out all across half a continent. Well, the dog may have had the more expensive lodging, but he didn't outdo us in the feelings department. No sirree! We felt fully as good as dogs when we got home.

Every Day Blind

Whenever I ride an elevator, I look at the interesting dots embossed on the operating panel and am reminded of Louis Braille, one of my favorite characters in history. Braille was born in 1809 in France. When three years old, he was blinded permanently in an accident. Not deterred by, but taking advantage of his blindness, at fifteen he invented the Braille system of six raised dots that have allowed blind people for over two centuries all over the world to read with their fingertips. Braille was also a dedicated teacher and a talented organist. When he died of consumption, his right hand was kept in Coupvray when the rest of him was borne triumphant to the Pantheon for burial.

Not to seem patronizing, but what would Braille have done with his life had he not been blind? And what could he have accomplished if he had been bitter about his affliction?

"Close your eyes," we are told as children. If we are also told to extend our hands, a toy may be forthcoming. But if we are told only to close our eyes, we are likely being prepared for a set piece of magic, for a story. Or it may be otherwise. My father told of an incident where he learned the imminent peril of being blind:

We lived in the country. One day my dad and mother went into town and let me go along. I don't remember all the things we got but there's one thing that I shall never forget. We saw an old man crossing the street slowly with a walking stick in front of him. I inquired and was told that he was blind and was feeling his way along with that cane. When we got back home, I had the job of bringing in wood from the yard. I was so impressed with the blind man feeling his way along that I got me a stick and tried it. Our porch was high above the ground. I was tapping my way, with my eyes closed, and then I fell off the porch and broke my left arm. I did not try that act again. I learned the value of keeping my eyes open.

"Close your eyes," we are told as adults. "Go back to an earlier time," the hypnotist murmurs. "Seek the larger life within you," says the leader. "Let us pray," intones the priest.

What is that place the sighted are bidden to evoke on a voluntary and temporary basis for moments of receiving magic, healing, enlightenment? What can we know from those who call this darkness home? Behind the scared, litigious-mindful, politically correct term "differently abled" is the true possibility of the sighted learning from the blind. Stealing from the blind—most odious of crimes—and yet we sighted might do just that, and without the blind feeling the loss one bit.

The late Ernestine Sewell, a Texas writer of note, told this story from her childhood in a letter to me:

At the entrance to the federal building and post office in Texarkana, where I grew up, a blind man sat day in and day out selling pencils. My mother always gave us coins for him. We made a game of trying to trick him (though we never gave him slugs as did some of the kids). It was a game to hand him a coin and watch him finger it, then drop it unerringly into a separate container for a penny, dime, quarter, half dollar, silver dollar, etc. He had a box for foreign coins.

Our delight in his showmanship was of course an inference that, because he was blind, he had to be mentally deficient. How ignominious for him!

And how might we glimpse what they have, what blooms in ingenuity and practicality, in humor, solitude, wisdom or beauty from this other human reality? Every day blind, every moment of life without sun or moon. What the pleasure, the pain?

How to get cigarettes, a promotion, the right colored purse for the shoes, the coffee hot, across the street, a lover, dill pickles only, the die in the clamp, the type proofed, the dog into church, the committee to work, the saddle on the horse, the bolt in the aperture, the envelope in the mail, friendship without condescension, closeness without burnout, patience without desperation, the job without pity.

"Light bothers me a lot," Gwen says, blind at 27 from retinitis pigmentosa. In that complaint the blind and the sighted may have common ground, except that it is the flotsam and jetsam the seeing receive in the light that may "bother" perception.

"I have a better life now than I did when I had my sight," says George, blinded by a gunshot wound in the face from a stranger. "I am happier...now life and the whole world mean a lot to me." How can this be? we ask, barred as we are from George's world. We follow him to work on public transit; we watch while he shops for groceries, kibitzes with relatives, goes to a bar on Saturday afternoon; we listen to his accounts of escapades into romance. Is this a person who, as the brilliant researcher Louis Cholden put it, has died "as a sighted person in order to be reborn as a blind man"?

"I've thought more about my hands since you asked me," Leonard, a 67-year-old blind horseman says. "See here how I run my hand down the back leg of my horse, getting ready to lift his foot. He knows my hand. It's not just any hand. You better not try it. I'm glad you asked me about my hands."

How to be alert but not nervous, wary but not paranoid, wise but not jaded, engaging but not boring, independent but not difficult, active but not foolhardy, proud but not haughty, lonely but not depressed, happy but not foolish.

If we listen and look past the pathology and the sociology of the blind, if we note with care their everyday acts: the peculiar sublimity of echolocation head movements; the way the hands combine power and delicacy when they touch objects, fingers curving upward and outward; the commingling of amusement and disgust on the brow of one sensing misjudgment; the quietude of posture in the concentrating worker—if we note these things, maybe that is enough. Enough for the sighted to be shown a world of strange beauty. Enough for the blind to say, "I'm glad you asked me about my hands."

This is every day blind.

III. Origins

Safe in the Arms of Trainmen

She was Lana Turner and I was Hedy Lamarr when the train went by. The rest of the time, we splashed about, with hopes of getting properly wet in her twelve-inch-deep concrete swimming pool, née watering trough. The pool was at the foot of her long sloping backyard, a kind distance from her mother's ears but not out of sight of a watchful eye from the kitchen window.

We were seven and eight years old, my friend Priscilla and I, both very white dishwater blondes growing up in that small north Texas town. Our suits were not Barbee bikinis, no spandex, no Day-Glo colors. They were one piece, colored burnt orange and royal blue, held up by a tie around our necks sometimes defaulting to allow an innocuous nipple to ride over the rim of the décolletage.

But already we were trying out our skills as "glamour pusses." When that first woof-woof came drifting down the tracks, we stopped what we were doing and prepared for the passage of the Katy some few yards away. We dipped our hair in the water and slicked it back, stood up and patted our soggy suits, clamored out of the water and perched, one on each of the back corners of the pool, like a couple of Acropolis porch maidens. Though we didn't know to suck in our bellies, the rest of us was ready—bony little feet angled, one knee provocatively bent, one hand on a hip, the other couching a head tossed back wantonly.

When the train finally made the California Street crossing, blasting full away at its stiff warning and proceeded south, the click of the rails drowning out any other reality, we began to giggle like crazy.

For we were doing something forbidden. We held our poses for the engineer and his assistant, sitting high up with their blue caps and red neckerchiefs in the cab of the engine. Yes, we wanted their eyes to pry, to think us beautiful candidates for true love, always, of course, just beyond reach. And sometimes we did indeed catch them. Sometimes they would flirt back—or so we thought—with a couple of friendly riffs on the whistle as they charged on down the track.

Then came the challenge of the people in the passenger cars. Now our hand on the hip was assigned to wave, condescendingly, of course, like a pretty beauty queen, not giving over too much heart or heat.

After the heads in the windows blurred by, we'd hop from our posts, traverse the cockleburs to the edge of the track bed, and stand rapt, counting, always counting, as though our lives depended on the correct number. The rattling, dizzying cars holding "c" things—coal, cattle, cotton, chemicals, construction—sped past us. We screamed the count into the chaos, glad for momentary relief of inhibitions imposed on us as nice little girls.

When we sensed a slackening of the din, we'd prepare ourselves for the caboose man. Was he the lowest in the hierarchy? Did he have official duties? We never knew what his job was, except to stand holding the back railing, surveying the receding scene and waving to us.

With him, we ladies of innuendo, we scandalous vamps turned virtuous, our ruse was over. To be sure, we had had about all the excitement we could manage. So we stood, hoarse and shivering now, a little pigeon-toed and pot-bellied, waving our sweet little hands to this uncle of a fellow, this last chance at daring contact with men.

About that same time, there were two other safe men at the scene of a train. On the shoulders of my father, in the summer of 1948, I see the only President I have ever seen, before or since, in person. Harry S. Truman is on his famous whistlestop tour, barnstorming the country, standing where the caboose man usually stands. This time it's called "the rear platform" and it's flag-draped.

Leaning forward, I yell into my father's ear, "He waved at me." My hands grip the crown of his head, my starting-to-be-long legs yoke his Old Spice neck.

"That's nice," he murmurs upward, "but pipe down."

"No, you don't understand," I say urgently, this time cupping his chin in my hand in a play for full attention. "He looked at *me, me!*"

"Oh, all right," my gentle father says quietly "Yes, I think I saw him do that."

And I wiggle a little, satisfied. For what more could a train ask, than to bring a girl's father and her President into perfect narcissistic alignment for her?

Another time, just before I drift off. My mother and I are going somewhere on a Pullman. The porter, tall and pure black, with pink palms that my blue eyes cannot quit staring at, has boosted me into an upper berth. Strange, he's done it so aseptically that it's as though he's not even touched me. Still, I lie there honored, flattered, feeling delicate and rich. Then he's said, "Goodnight, little lady," and drawn the curtains, taking my brown oxfords off somewhere to be shined like a princess's before morning.

The scene is a far cry from my maternal grandmother, Dora Pearl Bell, riding the train from Tupelo, Mississippi to Clarksville, Texas in 1895 as a seven year old. The family had had a hard winter, with nothing to eat but sowbelly and beans, and her father determined to give it a go in Texas. The womenfolk and children were in the passenger car, up front, while the men and boys were two cars back, with the cattle and household goods. If they kept the windows closed, the air was suffocating with body odors and tobacco, as well as stifling hot in the southern humidity. With the windows open, the woodburning engine belched ashes and cinder on them.

I do not think my grandmother had any train flirtations. I hope she had safe men on her train.

By the time I knew of trains, I knew of the dangers of certain men. So why do the trainmen, all of them, chug in and out of my memory as such wholesome personages? For one thing, they were public figures, to be trusted like policemen and postmen. They wore uniforms; they had hats. And they were kind to us kiddies, parasites forever waving alongside their tracks. They thrilled us with their whistles, and most of the time they bothered to raise their big worn hands to return our greetings. We could prance, preen, flirt, try all our instinctual wiles on them, and there was no chance they would stop the engines and come down to "get us," whatever that might mean.

And they had power. They operated those screaming, blasting behemoths up and down the land, dragging miles of cars, in a display of muscle that was so far from the domain of girl dreams that it seemed, at the least, the job of Assistant God.

And what of the other men in my life, hubbed around the memory of trains? The gentlemanly black porter, with more elegance than salary; my father, heaving his daughter up on his shoulders after a long wait on the brick-inlaid depot yard to afford her a glimpse of a President he roundly disliked; the same Harry S. Truman on his Presidential tour who waved at *me*, just an ordinary American girl, gosh!

They were all, all of them, honorable trainmen.

Gracious! Mercy!

I stood beside the grave of Barbara, who had died of cancer after only months of illness. A scholar, teacher, businesswoman, mother, and wife, she had shocked the entire community by slipping away.

I had a huge lump in my throat and my hands shook as I held my flute. In a safe moment over the phone with her husband, I had agreed to play "taps" for my friend. Now I wasn't sure I could do it. My grief was about to swamp me.

All was quiet, all eyes and ears waiting. Suddenly, from a nearby tree a raucous Great-tailed Grackle called out loud and clear. It made me and everyone else smile. I relaxed and began to play "Amazing Grace." People joined in singing. Grace, our unmerited favor from the Universe, surely comes in a myriad of ways.

My grandmother was a caller-on of grace. In moments of surprise, dismay, or delight, she would intone the variation on the concept, "Gracious!" and shake her hands a bit in front of her. I don't think I ever questioned exactly what that meant but it must have implied a plea for grace from her God, that God would help her withstand, or enjoy, or take in the shock of whatever she was confronted with.

"Gracious me!" was "Mercy me!" wearing a lace collar. Sometimes "Gracious me!" was a kind of stylized signal that she had an opinion about the situation and would further share it if I asked her. And often the opinion was about me or my cousins. When it was pronounced, you could feel your bad conduct at the dinner table—giggling, hunched over your food improperly, smacking—being reproved. Such would go down in the Book of Life, or at least in a whispered report to your parents upon their return.

"Mercy me!" with its alliterative slowness was more personal but less serious than just "Mercy!" The word by itself was reserved for an exclama-tion, for example when Mammaw caught a cuptowel on fire, or received the news that a neighbor's child had choked on a hard-boiled egg. It was accompanied by a look heavenward in supplication to the Almighty.

"Mercy me!" could be murmured over and over while shelling peas on the back porch with a neighbor. It could be used in reply to a bit of gossip about another neighbor. As a lack of endorsement, it could mean, "I'm listening to this juicy bit but don't necessarily believe it or agree to pass it on." It could also mean, "There's obviously nothing we can do, but we wouldn't even if we could."

"Goodness gracious!" could happen too. It had that same specific multisyllabic slowdown as "Mercy Me!" Some specific heeding would usually follow after that, like "Goodness gracious! You're not going to go outside barefooted in this weather, are you?"

When I think back on my Arkansas grandmother's use of "Goodness gracious!" and "Mercy Me!" I am reminded of an explication of an utterance in Psalm 23, the Good Shepherd psalm. "Surely goodness and mercy shall follow me all the days of my life," the psalmist avers. I once heard a unique interpretation of Goodness and Mercy by a highly creative evangelist. He explored the possibility that these two essences were the names of the herding dogs of the Good Shepherd, perhaps ancestors of our famed Border Collies. So it is "Here, Goodness!" "Here, Mercy!" that follow me doggedly in meaning and memory each time I confront that passage.

My Epton grandmother lies on a hillside in Southern Arkansas, long gone from the hard life of bearing seven children and being the obedient wife of a Landmark Baptist preacher. When I think back on her use of "mercy" and "grace," I hear her words connecting to the Scriptures. If we admit to needing mercy, we admit to imperfection, the awesome task of being human. If we embrace the idea of grace, we may call it by other names, like serendipity or happenstance. Whatever, it's there at times, to be marveled at and grasp with appreciation.

Fire, Earth, Air, Water

I remember the morning light, pale, welcome, moving into my sister's and my bedroom. I remember my father coming quietly into the cold room, the scritch! scritch! of the match on the back of the clay-back stove, the hum of the gas, the split second of anxiety when he doesn't know if there will be ignition, or if he will have to huff out the match and begin all over.

But most times it lights, a positive whoosh, with the flame expanding equilaterally to the clay grates on either side of the middle point where he's inserted the match.

My father stands.

I pretend to be asleep, not really in a devious way, just as a gift to him being allowed to waken me.

He goes to the foot of my bed and carefully takes my waiting blue flannel robe. Now he returns to the stove and holds it over the radiating heat.

In a moment he will call my name, "Jannie, oh Jannie girl. Are you in there?"

I'll consciously move, yawn, stretch, mumble a good morning. Off the covers. A shiver as I cross the cold wooden north Texas floor. I go to my father, turn my back to him and grasp the cuffs of my pajama sleeves. When I am ready he whisks my robe from the rising warmth and helps guide my arms into the sleeves.

Then he does the thing I love best. He *enfolds* me. Leaning over me, the smell of coffee and Old Spice predominant, he takes the sides of my robe and overlaps them across my front, tying the sash securely, and in a final gesture, presses me against his sturdy body, his arms encircling, his big hands briefly patting my eight-year-old belly. Some mornings, when he's in a playful mood, he will very gently scrub his overnight whiskers against my face. In all the years since, I have never had a better awakening.

Yet there was another awakening with my father and fire, not nearly as charming. When Dad was a pastor in Gainesville, Texas, he was cleaning our kitchen stove one day when a valve slipped off the pilot light.

A huge flame shot up to the ceiling, threatening to engulf the whole parsonage in a short time. Mother screamed. I suppose I screamed too, as I was standing in the door-way of the kitchen.

By sheer dint of will power, Dad took the malfunctioning part and, reaching barehanded into the flames, reattached it, thus quelling the fire and averting a disaster. His hands were burned badly enough that he had to be in the hospital a day or two. He came home with them bound in white gauze mitts which he would have to wear for several weeks. But he insisted on preaching that next Sunday. Today I have in my mind's eye a picture of him standing there in the pulpit with these two big white fists propped up on either side of the lectern, his Bible placed before him at the correct passage, preaching away.

Many years later, I remember holding Dad's hand while we sat on a bench outside his assisted living residence, sunlight warming his old bones. "Daddy," I said, "your hands look just fine, no scars even after that awful time when you burned them fixing our stove." He looked far off and smiled, "I don't remember that, but if you say so."

We are told that our personal memories are all stored in our bodies, that each cell contains the whole of our life experiences. It's the accessing of them that troubles our aging brains. In other words, it's not the memories that are gone, only our faulty recall of them. Maybe that is why it is necessary for children to write down what they remember of their parents' stories.

I am looking right now at a short blue-gray nylon jacket with a zip front that I have brought out from a closet. The label says, "Tailored for McGregor 100% DuPont Nylon." It has inside pockets and underarm eyelets. It's a size 40. It was given to my father by some grateful parishioner and is at least 62 years old. My father always wanted a son but when he was resigned to not having one, he capitulated to his two daughters, who asked in their teen years of the 50s if they could borrow his bomber jacket, dubbed "The Drizzler" because it was so...well, *nylon,* and could be worn in damp weather. The important thing was that it was James Dean *cool.* We rolled up our blue jean pant legs, rolled up the sleeves of Dad's McGregor jacket, and rolled off to some teen gathering with our boyfriends.

I wish I knew who had given the jacket its stains—a few little blobs the color of rust (blood?), some streaky grease spots. There's a tiny melted place near the zipper—probably ash from a boyfriend's cigarette. The coat is still presentable from a distance. Actually, it looks respectable enough that I could wear it when I take my neighborhood walk. I will not be putting it on e-bay any time soon, although there are some look-alikes there, from $39 to $5,000. You see, it's one of those hyper-ordinary keepsakes that causes a visceral feeling of love for my dad to course through me every time I look at it. I'm not taking a picture of it and putting it in the Goodwill sack. I might need to hug it to me the way my dad hugged me on a cold morning. It's hanging around, as long as I do. It's an ordinary charm.

The week we buried our dad was a cold bleak one in north Texas. He died on Tuesday evening after a sleet and snowstorm had coated the hapless unprepared area. By Saturday, the day of the funeral, the snow had turned to icy puddles.

I had always abhorred the practice of leaving a loved one lying in a coffin on artificial grass under a tent, for gravediggers to put unceremoniously in the ground and throw dirt over. "You'll be late for the luncheon at the church," my sister said, as I told her I wanted to stay until Dad was in the ground and covered up.

So I stood, with my family surrounding me, and watched while the workers came forward and with a back hoe and chain cradle, encased my dad's coffin in the concrete vault and lowered all into the earth. My immediate family and I stepped forward and threw roses on to the dome of the encasement.

But just as the vault should have come to rest, it began to sway back and forth. After a few moments, the motion stopped but in its place, water gushed from the sides of the grave. The coffin had displaced a hole full of water.

I thought of my dad's serene expression in death, of the little New Testament I had impulsively tucked into the crook of his arm, of his beautiful red tie, his best shirt. Despite knowing his spirit had gone, I was totally dismayed by the prospects of his coffin being filled with water. I was angry with the funeral home for not waiting a few days until the water level went down in the cemetery. No wonder they had tried to talk me out of staying!

I couldn't quit being troubled by the thought of Dad in his cold wet grave. Later that evening, I called my brother-in-law aside in the kitchen and told him what had happened. "Yes, I know," he said. "The funeral director was sorry about that. But it's like this," and Edward took a glass and inverted it in the dishwater. "Do you see the glass filling up?"

I had to admit I didn't.

"The vault created a vacuum that didn't allow the water to get any farther."

"Maybe so," I murmured, more to satisfy him than being really convinced. I went home still troubled.

Several weeks later I was bent over my periwinkles in the side garden, thinking of my dad, my heart still heavy with sadness and longing. A car pulled up and gave a little toot. It was my friend Don, the inveterate Saturday morning garage sale cruiser. I hadn't seen him in months. How had I been? he wanted to know.

I told him I'd lost my dad, and then, because it was still pressing on my mind, I told him the story of the casket *launched* in place of a dry burial. It was bizarre, I said, and I couldn't quit obsessing over it. Somehow, I felt I'd let my dad down by allowing that to happen.

Don listened quietly, and there, with me leaning on his car, my face streaked with dirt and tears, he said, "Jan, don't you see? It was perfect, If we're ashes to ashes and dust to dust, we're also water to water. The water of birth and the water of death. Your dad went to his final earthly baptism."

And with those words, my burden lifted. Through a casual Saturday morning conversation with my friend Don, I was led out of an obsessive grief.

So that's the water of my father's time on earth. The fire, both the warmth of a space heater and the potential destruction of our house from a kitchen gas stove, these he actively met and conquered. But what about the "Earth" and the "Air" in the title? Well, nylon is made out of coal and petroleum mixed with air and water into a polyamide. Let that count for the beloved bomber jacket he allowed us to appropriate and wear to our hearts' content.

I'm not sure what it all means...maybe that the most physical basic elements are the things memories hang themselves on. Maybe that all stories hearken back to the stuff of simple substances.

I will intone the old medieval elements—fire, earth, air, and water—as an incantation calling up my father. A warming fire on a cold morning, a daring flame, a nylon jacket made of coal and air, a friend's metaphor of watery birth and death—these I will explore, voice, cling to. The elements may, in the long run, tell of our most sacred longings.

Jan Seale

On the Home Front

I was four days old when Hitler invaded Poland on September 1, 1939.

I often reflect on how World War II was the norm of my life for the first six years. War was my cradle, my teacher, the color of conversations in our home. Ration books fascinated me. Scrap drives were exciting. I didn't know what caissons were but I knew they were rolling along in the song I sang with my playmates. A family joke is how I remained seriously frightened about "the draft" getting me, particularly when my mother came to close the window because "There is a draft."

A few years after I was born in Pilot Point, Texas (which carries the distinction of having the first bank robbed by Bonnie and Clyde) my family, consisting of my mother, father, my older sister Nan, and me moved to Gainesville, another north Texas town situated on the Red River, a few miles south of the Oklahoma line. Outside Gainesville was a large Army infantry training center, Camp Howze. Here green recruits came for basic training of a few weeks, to be shipped out to one or another "overseas theatre"—another war term confusing to a small listening child.

We often were stranded downtown by the passage of miles-long convoys shipping out or going on maneuvers. Several thousand soldiers were processed here over the course of the war. On occasion I went to Camp Howze with my father, a Baptist minister, when he was called to hold religious services.

During those years, my father officiated at dozens of weddings held in our home. In a time when lovers waited to sleep together until the knot was tied, the couples were eager to legitimize their love-making before the groom was shipped out. On wedding nights, my sister and I would sneak in our pajamas to the dining room, closed off from the living room by French doors. Lying on our stomachs and lifting the curtain ever so stealthily, we could see the seams on the nylons of the bride, the high-heeled ooh-lah-lah shoes. We craned our necks up, up to the taffeta or crepe dress with the peplum and butterfly sleeves, to the perky little pillbox of a hat above the netted snood. Oh yes, and the groom was slender, in military dress of pukey green, with shiny shoes, hair over-cut, and red ears slick with scrubbing.

Once I sneezed, giving away our voyeurism, and that ended our romp for that night. But it later provided amusement to family and friends, as our father made a clever anecdote out of "the night the French doors sneezed."

Our gracious mother often furnished a little bouquet of yard flowers for the bride and played "Here Comes the Bride" on the piano. Afterward, if she could manage it, there were slices of coconut cake and red punch. But of course by this time, my sister and I had raced back to our beds, regaling ourselves with what we had seen until we fell asleep.

It would be a long while before I understood that often, within a few weeks' time, my dad would be asked to go to the train depot to meet the funeral car carrying the coffin of the groom.

After serving as a prison for German prisoners of war, Camp Howze was dismantled. Today there is nothing left except a few chimneys and water towers and some fields covered with cement standards, row on row, that served as foundations for the buildings. On first glance, these blocks standing alone in rows look like tombstones, as well they might.

Even as a small girl, I think I sensed something of tremendous importance taking place on those wedding occasions. My mother and father seemed artificially cheerful on those nights. Now I know: they were eager to provide a little romantic assist to a couple of young people desperate to taste life, in case the present was all they would get.

Of Margarets and Aging

Seventy-seven. There. I said it. It's what I am in years. Two new tests have come about lately that make me more fully understand the implica-tions. Cashiers at fast-food places are more and more prone to give me the senior discount without asking. Yet in an adverse way, my ego has been saved by the new rule on people over 75 not having to take off their light jackets and shoes at airport security checks. It makes my day when a security person barks at me to divest and I get to say sweetly, "But I'm over 75." Still there's a downside to this—several times I've been sent to the pat-down line because "Honey, we can't tell what you have there under that jacket, and then there's all your jewelry."

Lately I have been thinking about this time in life I find myself living in. I have been thinking about how my children and grandchildren are *not* thinking about this time in life for me, or them. They are going about living—making money, having fun, aware acutely of what others are thinking and saying about them. They are chairing committees and planning what they will have for supper and accompanying their children to scouts and asking about homework and stopping by the electronics store to get a cord. I once did all these things.

I live in an area which receives thousands of "snowbirds" each winter, mainly older Midwestern people retired from farming and other life work who are seeking a warmer climate for several months of the year. They are free of their hometown obligations and bent on having fun, eating food at great RV park potlucks, and resting their callused hands from a half-century of work. Some of them turn to doing what their children have urged them to do, that is, writing down the stories of their lives which they have told orally X number of times at dinner tables. For over twenty years I taught a class in writing one's life story for these people at a local history museum. I called attention to the fact that they were in a life review, that we all had the urge to eternalize ourselves. They either liked the fact that their actions had labels or rejected out of hand this sentimental jargon.

When I first began teaching autobiographical writing and for a number of years following, I was amused by some of the behavior of these folks. On days when I wore a sweater, they wore shorts. Some of the women had slightly fried gray hair, a result of saving money at the local cosmetology college. They eschewed earrings and makeup in general. They wore exclusively no-iron polo shirts and clunky tennis shoes. They laughed loud, showing coffee-stained teeth, and were inordinately interested in where their classmates were from and what their occupation had been. In other words, they were being their authentic selves.

I, on the other hand, made sure my makeup was as perfect as possible (that is, okay—for a badly nearsighted person), selected earrings that did not sway and jiggle when I talked (so irritating to the listener, I reasoned) and wore tasteful color-coordinated outfits. When I said, "Please get out your paper and pen and number one through twenty, skipping every other line," I couldn't understand why one or two would invariably ask, "How many did you say to number?" or "Do we skip two lines or one?"

Now, *now*, I understand. Now, at 77. Now, when I do not multitask well and can remember only one thing at a time. There's nothing like the simple act of staying alive to make one eat crow.

Lately I have been living in the things-I'd-do-differently department. It's not that I've made huge mistakes that ruined other people's lives, that is, not that I know of. And I'm not exactly torturing myself with my memorable faux pas. It's just a clearing of vision, a remarkable stripping away of illusions that has hunted me down, taken me by the throat, and made me say Uncle, or rather Mother.

My mother spoke her mind right down to her last breath at 93. My sister Nan and I often found ourselves on the receiving end of her pronouncements and did the thing that grown children do—answered back. We came to find ourselves against practically everything our mother espoused.

No, we did not want to wear the clothes of hers she didn't want any more. No, we could not eat the stale or moldy leftovers she pressed upon us when we visited. No, we did not believe one cousin would meet his fate on his motorcycle because he was not attending church regularly. No, it wasn't the worst day of her life, as she declared it was, at my Thanksgiving table when she felt too hot as a result of wearing a polyester blouse with kitty-cat neck bow.

It was as though these outlandish things made us allergic to everything she said. We found ourselves infuriated when, with a little perspective, we might only have been irritated, even amused. I see now that we over-reacted to her other more charming and wise behaviors.

When I sit on my bed massaging Jergens Lotion into my feet, I wish I had offered more often to cream her feet when I went to see her in the assisted living home.

When I turn the covers back on my bed at night and crawl gratefully in, I know now why she took such pleasure in lying a-bed reading the newspaper and listening to the radio.

When I stay indoors all day in air-conditioning in our steaming tropical climate, I understand why she did not want to go on picnics when we visited her with our family in the summertime.

When I struggle to thread a needle, I am at a loss to understand how she could salvage the menswear material from my father's worn suits to make beautiful pencil-skirt, box jacket outfits for me to wear through college. When I am on the receiving end of stabbing pain in one pinky finger I forgive her for saying a loud "Oh!" in the middle of a conversation when her arthritis was acting up.

So it goes.

In altercative conversations with my sister Nan and me, Mother would often explode into anger and shake her knotty forefinger at us: "Just you wait! You'll come to this someday!" And sure enough, we have.

Sunday afternoons at four Nan and I have our weekly phone talk. These conversations sometimes last until five-thirty or six, much to the chagrin of others who want to talk to us *right now*. A good portion of our conversation lately has been rehashing our lives with our parents. Dad lasted until 88, Mother to 93, and Nan and I are senior-age orphans realizing that they are truly gone, absent in a way we never believed that—when they were alive and we were obsessing over their quirkiness—we could miss them.

We laugh about Mother's last words on her deathbed: "Don't throw away that plastic bag!" About how she was the queen of weather, calling me each time she knew I was starting out on a cross-country trip with the admonition to be sure to take my winter coat because "there's a front coming from the east and another from the west, and the north and south don't look too good either."

Then there was the memorable occasion when we took our parents simultaneously to their respective doctors, who happened to be officed on opposite sides of the same building. When they had finished their visits and we were loading them—purse, cane, walker, sacks of pills, hat, etc.

etc.—into the car, I whispered to Nan, "You won't believe what Dad said in his waiting room." She countered, You won't believe what Mother said in *her* waiting room."

After depositing them at home, we confided in the garage. My sister went first: "The waiting room was filled with people. To keep down conversation, I was trying to read. Mother picked up a newspaper and in a minute asked loudly, 'How does that husband of yours like Viagra?'"

I countered with my story. Dad's waiting room was packed, and several had spoken to him already, people in his past pastorate who mentioned how he as the reverend had married them, or buried their kin, or counseled them about family problems. After a while he got restless and said, for all the room, "It's a good thing I don't have a gun; I'd fix myself." This, from a man who spent his life directing other people to the good non-violent life and to a heaven ever after.

My sister and I were more lenient with our dad's foibles than we were with our mother's. Still, when I'd go to visit, I'd find pathetic notes in his handwriting all over the house, ones that said perfectly obvious things, like "Jan will be here at 6 p.m. Tuesday unless her plane is late." Now the surfaces of my house are littered with notes—bedside, kitchen counter, refrigerator, desk. These notes include notes noting where I have put notes.

I vacillate between accepting my age and wanting to deny it. Okay, so one of the hazards on the list of old age is losing the ability to make a decision. The e-mails of my round-robin "copy to all" groupies from high school are full of doleful accounts, mine included, of our latest physical status. Seems *health* is our news. There are those whose arthritis is acting up, who have pinched nerves and numb hands, high blood pressure, and faulty heart valves. And then we begin the report on our husbands, three of whom have passed on, and the living ones suffering from prostate cancer, clogged arteries, and dementia. We have always vowed we'd get together once a year, but that hasn't happened for several years.

A couple in our group are adept at finding on the internet funny disgusting lists beginning "You know you're old if..." I detest these and love them, alternately, depending on what kind of day I'm having when I receive them. From time to time I propose to myself an age-free day where I will not talk about, read about, or think about aging. There will be no medical comparisons, no reading of medical newsletters, no listening to radio doctor call-ins, no commiserations with broken hips or wrists. And there will be no "I don't remember's" or rolling eyes accompanied by "Old age is not for sissies." Obviously, as I write, this is not one of those days.

The other topic of conversation in my circle of age-enhanced friends is travel. I have been to one too many dinner parties where all the attendees have been to Africa except me. And so for two hours, I listen to itineraries, near misses on wildlife (either with camera or gun), and the merits of a favorite lodge. My financial adviser asks me each time I go in for a consultation what trips I have planned, as if there is no life for elders outside of packing up and flying off on a tour. I finally told him we'd had a great time fixing up our yard and buying a car.

I was hooked in recently by a side bar on the internet to learn "Five tips on makeup for older women," this from a model with ravishing silver hair, large moony eyes, and high cheekbones. The tips all pointed to "less is more." Yeah, I thought, say on.

Still, I like what has happened to women's fashions since our grandmothers' days. "Age-appropriate" is right up there with other bleeped words. Every now and then, I stop to think about what my grandmothers were wearing when they were my age. Black orthopedic lace-up shoes and flowered housedresses were the order of the day, with plenty of under-garments including long-line bras and corsets. Neither of my grandmothers ever drove a car and one did not ever cut her hair. One Sunday recently I wore leggings, wedge-heeled shoes, and a blouse with leather sleeves. Whoopee! My sister, who is my fashion adviser and a bit older than I, has only lately sworn off ruffles and loud colors.

I've tried placing my silver tea service and assorted silver-plate platters with a high-end consignment service, only to be told to come get them after three months. So now, when I can't stand their tarnish any longer, and in memory of the dear departed contemporaries of my mother who gave them to me as wedding presents in 1958, I polish them as an exercise for my upper arms, which have not been defying gravity lately.

Who are my models for aging? In a fit of serendipity, I realize that several are named Margaret. Most immediately, I think of my sister, whose name is actually Margaret Nan. She constantly inspires me with her optimism about life. In our Sunday afternoon phone conversations she tells me one time about helping at her local food pantry and another about playing veterinarian with her granddaughters under the dining table. It's a great comfort to me that there's a person who shares my parents with me. I look to her for cheer, stability, and, in these later years, the comfort of kin. She is a unique person, radiating beauty and personality.

I think of another Margaret whom we introduced to our good friend and widower Bob when they were in their 70's. We friends gave her a lingerie shower before they married and she modeled her baby-doll shortie pajamas for us—*over* her clothes. She had raised five sons with her late first husband. Now, with Bob, she delighted in preparing recipe delicacies—papaya conserve and venison back-strap and Mexican wedding cookies. She gave Scots-Irish toasts at parties, played the cello, and raised avocadoes. Margaret was outlandish and saucy-tongued. I loved her.

Present-day friend Margaret, who wore a gold lamé dress low-cut in the back revealing a flawlessly smooth back for her 80th birthday celebration, is too busy to be old. She seamlessly picks up grandchildren after school, serves on local- and beyond boards, travels with her husband, reads widely, and champions her friends' interests. This Margaret lost two of her five children tragically when they were young. She is beyond strong.

And then there is my own mother Margaret, whose shenanigans I have described earlier. But I must round out the portrait. She remains the most important Margaret in my life, the one I think about most as I age. With a strong resemblance to her, she is the ghost who greets me in the bathroom mirror when I get up at night.

Along with being a piece of work, my mother had many traits which I am proud to be descended from. She taught my sister and me the distaff arts. Not that we practice them like she did in her utterly necessary way, but Nan and I can sew, cook, entertain, and keep an attractive house. Between us, we have raised seven children and were married a combined total of 110 years. Mother Margaret nursed me through a bout of childhood tuberculosis when there were no lifesaving medications for it. She saw to it that we had piano lessons and pretty dresses. She served, without salary or recognition, alongside our father the hundreds of parishioners who attended the churches our father pastored.

Every holiday, and often in between, Mother sent us down the block to a small frame house where lonely old Miz Western lived. We carried a shallow cardboard box containing a plate heaped with our holiday fare, a double helping of dessert, and a small jar of tea or coffee. I never forgot the lesson. Today I maintain a supply of those cardboard boxes, named fondly our "sick and afflicted" boxes. They are just right for filling with a homemade meal for a lonely, sick, or bereaved household.

And then there were the hungry homeless men who knocked at our back door. We called them bums or tramps, without any compunction for political correctness. Their appearance was such a common occurrence that we didn't know to be afraid. Mother would deliver to them a huge plate of food, a fruit jar of tea, and a pamphlet on how to be saved. They would stuff the pamphlet in a pocket, sit down on the steps and gobble the food. I was feverishly curious about them so she allowed me to sit with them and observe, all the while keeping a keen eye on me from the kitchen. Imagine such a scene today, or don't.

Born in 1911, Mother was named Margaret Belle, the first daughter in a family of six children. In her family, she was known as Maggie Belle, as well as Sister, Sistoo, or Mugs. Her middle name was derived from her mother's maiden name, Bell, with an "e" added to connote femininity. She went through school with Choctaw children whose families had been relocated in southeastern Oklahoma in small towns where her father served as principal and teacher in their schools. After she graduated from high school, she taught with her father in the school she had attended earlier.

"Margaret" is the Greek word for "pearl." There are many variations, such as Greta, Marjorie, Peggy, even Rita. Meditating on the qualities of pearls, I am reminded of what the jeweler said when I took in an old strand of my mother's pearls, yellowed and thinly strung. "Treat them as antiques," he said. "Their color is precious."

The yellow glows with a deep penetrating color that echoes the pearls' history. Such is the memory of our mother Margaret—glowing forth as a competent young and midlife woman and descending into a cranky old yellow soul, to be treated in my sister's and my memories at long last as a beloved antique. We treasure her worth, her tarnish which now seems like shine, even as we ourselves take on the patina of old age.

My Mother's Buttons

Somewhere in the third world, women are walking about in buttonless blouses, their breasts more available for babies. Men in buttonless shirts flutter and flap as they walk the edge of garbage dumps. All the buttons are home in my mother's sewing box. They are arranged in plastic bags according to color.

Some bags are further subdivided into clustered sets.

What does it mean to leave behind a legacy of buttons, so many more than one could ever use? Ironically, there were no buttons, not a single one, on the dusty-rose chiffon we buried her in.

At the last, Mother just played with them, sifting through the sacks or dumping an entire bag on the bed to skewer similar ones on large safety pins. When I flew in for a visit, she would often gift me with a small miscellaneous sack of them to take home "just in case you need one."

In button collecting, Mother could focus on a tangible, if passive world—faces with two waiting, questioning eyes, or four holes playing a game with the thread, or no holes at all but a shank hiding in the back.

When she died, I could not bring myself to put the bags of buttons in the Soul's Harbor stack. With leisure to look at them in a sentimental way, I found some of my girlhood history: a two-toned covered button from a loved childhood coat, a set of glittery rhinestone eyes from a piano recital outfit, and little plastic fruit buttons from the front of a blouse made from flour sacks. The buttons triggered memories I hadn't any idea I was still walking around with. (If the neurobiologists are correct, I have button-memory in my knees, ears, and ankles.)

My father was represented there too, in leathery woven buttons from his sports jackets—large ones for the front matching smaller ones for the sleeves. Flat dumb-faced buttons from which suspenders were fastened on the inner waistbands of pants. Lions' heads. Anchors. Initials. Coats of arms. And a clan of white pearly cousins waiting to be sewn on abused dress shirts coming back from the laundry.

Buttons are metaphors for the exchange of cells on earth: ore, shell, cellulose, wood. Wildness and chaos stamped out—no doubt in factories where workers must dream up intrigues and fantasies to counter the

Jan Seale

boredom of mass production.

To my mother, buttons were stays against another Great Depression. True, she used her collection with vigor and practicality when she sewed for the whole family. But after that, in her waning years, they became a hedge against poverty. If there was no food, no money, nothing—at least she had her doggie bags of buttons. She knew she would never use them all, but she wanted to be prepared...to be able to find that exact aqua or orange or black without having to go to Walmart or Singer's.

And, like the factory workers who must wearily stamp them out, she needed her fix against the utter ennui of unraveling life. Long past the time of banquets and parties, she sewed shiny buttons on silver lamé dresses, to go with perfectly good silver pumps and a silver purse. She might be asked out, and she wanted to be ready.

Mother thought she had a corner on buttons but they are truly community property. Universally owned. They may be borrowed from the general hoard, for fastening this one's blouse, that one's pants, decorating this mirror, that couch pillow, but sooner or later they will drift back into the flotsam, becoming in the dust, symbols of our culture before their name was the same as that of devices on our machines ("Use the 'pause' button"). There are forerunners now of that coming age—strays in gutters, drawers, or nattering around in vacuum cleaners.

Microcosms of what is faithful, useful, bright, touchable, buttons can stave off loneliness and insanity. You can count, and count on buttons. As usual, Mother knew best.

The Respectability Factor

What do Denzel Washington, Jane Austen, Vincent van Gogh, Katy Perry and I have in common? We are the children of preachers. Someone has said you don't have to have a difficult childhood to be a writer but it helps. I didn't have a difficult childhood but mine was certainly different.

My father was a Baptist minister, the child of a Baptist minister. Had I been a boy, I might have been pressed into service myself. My sister Nan and I being girls didn't have much incentive to follow in our father's foot-steps. However, we were encouraged mightily to behave, not to do anything that would jeopardize Dad's position as an outstanding leader in the two communities in Texas where we spent our growing years.

The first Sunday of my father's tenure in Waxahachie, a small charming town south of Dallas, I made a definite impression on his parish-ioners. He and Mother had waited until the Christmas break to move us from our old school in Gainesville, up on the Red River, to the new one. That Sunday evening the choir was singing selections from Handel's *Messiah*. Dad was ensconced in an over-sized pulpit chair while my mother, Nan and I were sitting smack-dab in the midst of the sanctuary among an overflow crowd there for the special Christmas music. Just as the singers belted out "For unto us a child is given," I notified my mother that I was nauseated. She quickly gathered purse, coats and gloves and we began to climb over people to get out. I only made it to the center aisle and there divulged the contents of an enchilada lunch and chess pie onto the sacred carpet. The choir sang the Halleluiah chorus while the janitor, on hands and knees, removed the evidence. I was sick for a whole week and it was years before I could eat enchiladas. I still don't eat chess pie.

It was one of many acts on my part that countered the role of a member of a respectable preacher's family. Still, our parents tried. There were rules. We did not wear shorts in public; at home, we could wear them but had to don a skirt hurriedly if we answered the door. We did not dance; Mother said to go ahead if we wanted to be the cause of Dad's being asked to resign. We did not sit out in cars at night with boys in front of the parsonage; so we parked on country lanes with our boyfriends. We did not wear bright red lipstick or mascara; Dad said we looked like the side of a red barn.

No movies, shopping, or card-playing on Sunday.

We were to set an example—for what or whom I could not fathom, since most of our friends were moving right ahead with their sinning. I'll never know how many boyfriends I might have enticed had they not been afraid they'd go straight to hell if they got close to the preacher's daughter. It seems sex was completely outside the realm of possibility for a preacher's family. Indeed, one of my friends wondered aloud how on earth literally I had arrived on earth since my presence was testimony that my parents had "done it." That sort of thing? For a man and woman of God? Pillars of the community?

My sister and I spent many hours at the church, especially on Wednesday night for prayer meeting, and on Sundays, for Sunday School and morning worship, and in the evening, Training Union and evening worship. There were advantages to such delays in going home, (Catholics, close your eyes) one being that we were allowed to eat the tiny delicious unleavened leftover crackers and drink the grape juice from The Lord's Supper. Sated with the Elements, we might stretch out on a pew cushion and drift off to sleep as Dad was counseling some distraught soul who had lingered behind for free guidance.

As a minister's family, everything except groceries and clothes was pretty much free in a small friendly town in Texas. There were free piano lessons, free dry cleaning, free doctor and dentist, free haircuts. When my parents retired in Waxahachie, many years after my father's pastorate in that town, Mother could not understand why she had to wait thirty minutes in the doctor's office; after all, she was a preacher's wife!

Holidays in the manse were rife with floral arrangements. At Christmastime, the doorbell rang frequently with the arrival of poinsettias sent by parishioners and other friends about town. When the door closed, Mother would sigh, "We are running out of places to put these." (By this time, the dining table overflowed with hundreds of Christmas cards.) The same was true of lilies at Easter. When I grew up and created a home of my own, I was nostalgic for these flower-filled holidays, so my mother and father made sure I had at least one Christmas poinsettia and one Easter lily for our layperson house.

One woman in Gainesville who was single and owned the town's beauty shop doted on us. She was known only to Nan and me as Morris. One Christmas Morris outfitted us completely with lovely plaid skirts, matching wool jackets, patent leather shoes, felt hats, lacey gloves, and swinging purses. At Easter, we had eyelet-pique dresses with floppy hats, straw purses, and new sandals. Of course, there were free haircuts and permanents at her shop. I still remember screaming in terror when I smelled my own hair sizzling under the permanent wave machine clamped to my head. I suppose I appeared proper and cared for the next Sunday.

Looking back on those days, I believe "respectable" was the highest virtue that could be asked of a preacher's family. It was certainly the byword in our household. And it was not just at Sunday services that we were on display. We very often were invited to dine in the home of parishioners. We were expected to display exemplary manners for these occasions—no sitting on your foot, no fiddling with food, please and thank you, laugh at Dad's jokes.

One memorable occasion, we were to dine with a couple of spinster sisters who worked as telephone operators. The Martha of the two, definitely the alpha sister, scampered about putting the fried chicken and mashed potatoes on the table. When we were all seated, she asked the meek Mary if she would offer thanks. We all bowed our heads, there was a slight pause, and Mary murmured reverently, "Number please." Nan and I tried hard to suppress the giggles but as I recall, a sputter or two leaked out while Mary was changing professional hats and regrouping herself to say grace.

My sister and I survived the parsonage years partly because we were often made privy to what went on behind the scenes. The talk at the table was invariably about church doings. We worried, along with Dad, that he would let the plus-size new-Christian non-swimmer of a man slip out of his grip when he immersed him in the baptistery.

We laughed hilariously at the story of the old busybody who lived near the church and, upon looking in the door one Monday morning, called the police because she thought my father had hanged himself. They came rushing in to discover that he had hung his baptismal waders, identical to fishing waders, in a doorway to dry.

And we knew, and were sworn to secrecy, that Dad hated the tradition in one church during the Christmas season of erecting a huge orange neon angel spanning the area behind the pulpit, bubbling seductively behind him as he preached.

The part of the service in a Baptist church that still pains me in memory is the time of invitation when sinners were encouraged to come forward confessing themselves and accepting Christ as their Savior, new families in the community could come to join the church, young people could surrender to preach or be missionaries, and backsliders might rededicate their lives. At the end of the sermon, my father descended from the pulpit and stood in front of the communion table with Bible in hand as the choir and congregation rose to their feet and began singing in a soft whine "Just As I Am" or "Oh, Why Not Tonight?" Dad would smile and oscillate gracefully side to side, alternating hands gripping his Bible. I was reading him intently and he looked tense and uncomfortable. Once I asked my mother if Daddy would be happier if I would go down and surrender to be a missionary. To her credit, she said that wasn't nearly a good enough reason.

Mother avowed that she could always tell something strange was going on in the service when Dad's neck changed to a bright red against his white collar. That was frequently the case at the invitation. Later we would learn about the woman who came forward requesting money for her gall bladder operation. Another time a man surrendered to preach against life insurance. And one Easter, a young girl skipped down front to show Dad her new shoes and tell him she got a real live bunny for Easter.

These stories were recounted later at home with great hilarity. The serious respectability factor was often leavened with our father's sense of humor. Another thing I'm thankful for in retrospect was the value given to books and ideas. Our dad maintained a huge home library. True, there were many books of theology but there were also books of history and sets of encyclopedias and dictionaries. Magazines were plentiful: *Reader's Digest*, *Life*, and *Time*. And Mother subscribed to *Better Homes and Gardens* and *The Ladies' Home Journal*. We took *The Dallas News* and the hometown paper.

Cogent to all the reading opportunities at home, I am grateful to have had a thorough grounding in the Bible as literature. I know the stories of Noah, Isaiah, Esther, Matthew, Jesus, and Paul. When I am brought low, an encouraging verse, committed to memory in a long-ago Vacation Bible School, Sunday School, Training Union, or Girls' Auxiliary readily pops up on the board to argue with me about despondency. Even phrases in awful hymns (written about elsewhere in this collection) may make me smile and settle down. My friend Karol, who shares my Baptist background, told me recently that despite all her conscious sophisticated efforts, she arose some mornings with "Jesus wants me for a sunbeam" hammering away in her brain. I commiserated.

Sometimes Dad would take one of his daughters with him to visit in the homes of church members. When he had to call on a single woman, Mother wisely went with him, but when she was unavailable, we were pressed into service. It was only when I became an adult that I realized the necessity of our presence. There was too much risk of talk if the minister went to visit a woman home alone.

As was the case with most pastors, my father was on call 24/7, plus holidays. Once in the middle of the night when I was about eight, Mother was in the hospital when Dad got the call to go to the home of a church member who had just died. My sister Nan was spending the night with a friend. Dad woke me, rolled me in a blanket, put me in the car, and we drove to the residence. Parking directly in the doorway, he told me not to be afraid, tucked me in, and locked the car. I sat there in the dark for what seemed like ages, then began to rearrange my blanket. Darned if I didn't get on the horn! Dad came out in a flash.

A website labeled "Preacher's Kids International" is "dedicated to the celebration and recovery of those who grew up in the parsonage." From the vantage of over a half century, I think now there was more to celebrate than to recover from.

But of the disadvantages, I'd have to name the absence of my father, either physically or emotionally, too much of the time. It was only when he got old and disabled that we were able to talk heart to heart. In my growing years, he was busy or preoccupied with his job. And I resented when we had to stop a family vacation and drive home because someone in the church had unkindly taken to dying while we were trying to have fun.

We three women, my mother and sister and I, were there to keep him going. We washed his black socks in the lavatory by hand on Saturday mornings and ironed his starched shirts in the afternoon. Curiously, Dad was never the disciplinarian that our mother was. Maybe that was just the way they parceled out their duties—he left that chore to the mother of girls.

I knew that the church meant everything to him and Mother. Long before *Sophie's Choice,* but when I was old enough to hear about Hitler, I posited that if Hitler came and made my parents choose between their faith and me, they would choose the church. It never occurred to me to canvass them on the subject. Maybe I was too afraid. Once, I had a premonition that I was going to die in the night, so I went and told my mother. She said, "Well, you're a Christian, aren't you?" That was not exactly what I wanted to hear. I have a feeling that if they could read this confession now, they would shudder. We all change. We may all be forgiven our indiscretions as parents.

From a distance of over half a century, I sometimes think about my father and mother's lives—their dedication to a narrower and simpler way of seeing the Spirit and the soul. They were passionate about the church, the Baptist denomination, about being examples of virtue and respectability. And what was the outcome of my father's preaching the gospel for seventy years? I ask this now in a time when faith has transformed for many in our present age from "the gospel truth" to something either absent or much more complex. I try to remember that besides being the spiritual guide for hundreds in the community, Dad functioned also as a counselor, therapist, conflict manager, and psychiatrist in the town—not that these roles were superior to his pulpit presence but that they were applied faith, something that people needed imminently, could take home and implement right then, even though they knew they were "saved and going to heaven."

When my sister and I were young, Mother expended much energy to buy us narrow shoes. Triple A widths were hard to find and expensive. But she persisted, for she was filled with pride that we had slender feet. An old Southern idea postulated that only common people (who did fieldwork?) had wide feet. Mother wanted her girls to be known as ladies.

In Bible times, narrowness was given its due. There were close passes through mountains, undersized gates, and back alleys. All signified danger and the need for alertness. But there were treasures afterward.

My feet are not skinny anymore but I recognize other narrow aspects in my life. I need help in close calls of health, driving 2-lane roads, dense crowds, and work projects with a narrow time frame. What many would consider was a constriction, a narrowness in upbringing is something I am on friendly terms with. The only thing that I think of as permanently damaging: I didn't get to dance!

The list of celebs that were preachers' kids is long and deviant. Along with certain upstanding folk like Aretha Franklin and Ralph Waldo Emerson, we have Friedrich Nietzsche, a famed atheist, and Alice Cooper, a blood-spewing rock star. Obnoxious individuals are not excused by a devout upbringing. Neither is it right to blame scandalous behavior on a righteous heritage.

I was one of the lucky ones, child of a preacher father who never raised his voice at home, rather saving his volume for the climax of his sermon. Some of my best friends are P.K.'s and I wish every one of them a reconciliation—a coming-to-Jesus, if you will—with their heritage. Being a P.K. is a special baptism of background.

Of Sons and Ovaries

On the morning of surgery the temperature outside is two degrees Fahrenheit here in Rochester, Minnesota. At 6:00, we walk through a pastel carpeted tunnel connecting the hotel to the hospital. I have no purse. I don't wear my watch or ring. I have on no make-up. On either side, holding hands with me, are two of my favorite men, my 67-year-old husband and my 39-year-old son. Both are here to help me through a "procedure," as the medical community has dubbed the laity's old-fashioned "operation" or "surgery."

This is "*major* surgery," as I heard it used in my childhood. This is opening me up from stem to stern to remove a tumor, along with a uterus and ovaries with an expired use-by date, and to patch a hernia. Definitely major.

My husband Carl has come with me from South Texas to the Mayo Clinic to be a loyal support. Our son Erren has come to be the patient advocate and bedside nurse. He and I don't know how this is going to work, but since I don't have a daughter, and women friends are not free, we have to try the arrangement. On the plane, we agree that we're moving into unknown territory, that there are no instruction kits for this event. We also agree that we have to leave our inhibitions at home.

And what does Erren know about nursing? He majored in commer-cial art and is a successful businessman. Back in our hometown on the Texas-Mexican border, Erren co-owns Vida, an antique and cultural arts store. He lives 20 blocks from us, in a two-story stucco house surrounded by palms and bougainvillea. He has two brothers, both fathers and husbands, also with careers.

Why would I need Erren when my husband is coming with me? Carl has mid-stage Parkinson's Disease. He nods off a number of times a day, has waning strength, and cannot react quickly. My only sister and sibling is tending our aged parents back in Texas. My closest friend has a ski trip long planned with her family.

Can Erren do this intimate job? How will I feel about letting him? These things we don't know, but we're about to find out.

I wake up a few hours later with the same men holding my hands.

They bend to kiss me, say, "It was benign." Benign: the most blessed word in the language.

And then begins a series of days and nights all run together and shot through with a mix of pain, laughter, and problem-solving.

The black morphine trigger gets lost in the covers a half-dozen times a day and Erren is there to help me find it, laugh with me as I say, "Gimme that sucker!" and push it firmly to deliver niceness to my pained body. By day, he is in and out, tending to my needs. By night, he sleeps in the fold-down chair beside my bed.

We develop a routine. "I have to *go*," I say.

He begins unplugging from their outlets all the connections I am attached to. "Is it pee or poo?" he inquires, capping off my tubes, pinning them to my nightgown. Each time he asks, he makes me laugh, with these silly useful terms. Whichever, he adjusts his speed to the urgency. The IV pole must be changed to the other side of the bed, the bed lowered, and me assisted to my feet. We shuffle to the bathroom, he steadies me, positions the IV pole, and stands outside the door listening and waiting until I'm finished. Sometimes he hands a supply through the door. Sometimes he calls the nurse.

So we are working out what we thought might be hard for us.

For Erren's part, I marvel how he apparently intuits what a post-op, foggy-headed mother needs, and lovingly supplies it. Day by day, sailing uncharted waters, mother and son are discovering a new continent, a new way of *being* to each other.

We have changed places, at least for now. Like a parent, he nurtures, acts with authority, coddles and cajoles. I respond to his direction, laugh, at times am cranky and uncooperative, and end up feeling secure, cradled.

Among the hours of convalescence, there is time to talk, something we have not had in a couple of decades. Between words, we stare out the window at snowflakes drifting down, enjoying a weather event absent in our South Texas subtropics.

One day at sunset, Erren notices a huge flock of crows flying into town to roost in trees on the hospital grounds. And from then on, the three of us make a ritual of watching, waiting at sunset for the great sky-darkening throng.

And there is time to laugh. When a change of dressing reveals a swollen hump at the top of my incision in the middle of my diaphragm,

Erren promptly names the protrusion the "Boob-ette."

There are hitches in my recovery, and no mother-son handbook tells us how to respond. Some nights I vomit helplessly. I'm sure it couldn't have been any fun for him in the relay of the two aqua kidney-shaped pans between the bathroom and my retching. Those nights we are lucky to get an hour or two of sleep, before my digestive system acts up again. We figure out that I can doze off if Erren will reach his hand through the safety bars from his position in the chair by the bed and gently draw circles on my back.

When I develop a superficial infection in one of the drain tube openings on my right side, Erren bends over the site, working to get the tape to stick properly. When a new bag is attached to my IV pole, I hear him asking "What's this?" I hear him taking care of my insurance clearance, exchanging the orange juice for apple juice, and asking the doctor if I could be allergic to a medication. I hear him urging his father to go back to the hotel for the night. I relax. This grown son seems to know intuitively what it takes to nurture his mother back to health.

And as I write this, years later, I am thankful for the mysterious bonds between mother and son, for connections that don't end when the son is weaned, or goes off to college. With luck, the bonds reshape through the years, changing from simple bloodlines to overlays of love and experience.

Tweaked by a little magic and a lot of living, a mother and her adult child may become—the best of friends.

A Caregiver's Story
presented at the Caregivers Summit of the National Parkinson
Foundation
Sept. 19, 2016 in Portland, Oregon

Recently I flew from my hometown deep in South Texas to Houston, a short 50-minute flight. After we'd been told to prepare for landing, I noticed that the plane turned abruptly and seemed to be heading out to sea, over the Gulf of Mexico. Hmm, I thought. Hmm. As a poet, my imagination sometimes gets me into trouble. There had been some buzz on the news recently about hijacked planes and the D.B. Cooper incident up there in the Northwest.

But, in a few moments, my white knuckles turned back to pink when the pilot told us we'd be circling the airport for a while because Vice President Biden had landed in Houston and the airport was shut down until he cleared the area.

This experience is a lot like the caregiving one. Before the diagnosis, you and your loved one are flying along just fine, headed through the clouds, going someplace special and about to be there. Suddenly, Parkinson's comes along—and there's a sharp turn in the wrong direction, you're horrified that you're heading out to sea—you've been hijacked—disaster is imminent. And then comes the announcement: you are in a holding pattern. You will circle and circle and circle. Finally, you land. Things on the ground will not go precisely to plan. You may miss your ride, and you may be late for your meeting. But the point is, you are safe for now.

I happened to be married to a man who had Parkinson's for 20 years. Carl was a musician—an orchestra director, music professor, and composer. He conducted a mid-size regional orchestra in South Texas for 29 years, the last eight after his initial symptoms appeared. When he retired, he continued to compose music, using a rather elaborate computer music writing program. The day before he died, he asked to be taken to his computer...he had a little more editing he wanted to do. And that next afternoon, that long afternoon when he died, the helpers and I made sure he was listening to a recording of his own music.

Jan Seale

Parkinson's in some ways is a do-it-yourself disease. I don't mean that one should self-medicate or not follow doctors' advice. But very soon after diagnosis, we came to understand that because Parkinson's has such a broad span of manifestations, and because patients respond in such different ways, and because Parkinson's usually lasts a long time, it was up to us to be creative and pro-active.

From the beginning—those sneaky symptoms and then the diagnosis, my husband and I thought the worst thing was to feel helpless. We thought knowledge was always better than blind ignorance or denial. Intentions count. Plans count. Plotting counts. So we did things on our own: reading, looking up meds, participating in exercise and speech programs. We went to a nutritionist and began a program of supplements —which continued through the years and which, if he laid off a few days, he said he missed.

Notice I'm saying "we." There comes a time when you're so closely focused on the condition that you almost feel like you have it too! Sometimes my hands shook worse than his.

We determined not to be afraid of information, including that coming from doctors. When we could, we consulted neurologists specializing in Parkinson's. In that 20 years, we had three local neurologists, and others practicing in San Antonio, Houston, and Dallas. For a time, we made a thousand-mile round trip to Dallas to see a neurologist we learned about through a Parkinson's newsletter. His information was not radically different from that of others, but the 30 minutes with him, when he asked Carl about his life, his vocation and passions, then said, "Let's keep you doing what you love," that time with him was worth every mile to Carl.

We became bold about pressing medical people for explanations— "Say that again"— "Spell that please"— "I have two more questions on my list." Before Carl's open-heart surgery, we printed off info from the internet to show the anesthesiologist, who was not familiar with the interactions of a new Parkinson's med. We allowed one doctor a margin of error when he said back pain could not be a result of Parkinson's.

As the years went by, we became the king and queen of innovation. Medications and supplements kept stacking up, taking up too much space and time. We ended up grouping them into four main gulpings daily, and putting them into one large pill dispensary. Voila! We had some kitchen counter space and some respite from thinking about them all day. And, important for me, the caregiver, he could do them himself.

We said to hell with the fancy clothes of a professional man and went to pants with elastic waists, stretchy diabetic socks, and rubber shoes.

When we went out to eat—and this was high on our list of priorities —we took a large spoon for him, and a long apron that didn't show splotches and reached from his chin to his lap.

When a wheelchair became his choice of conveyance, we bought a van with a lift and took off on a vacation.

Choices were very important to us.

We were lucky that both of us had individual meaningful work. Carl composed on his computer. I wrote poems and stories.

A peculiarity of Parkinson's is a crop-up of obsessions, the brain begging for certain things. A preoccupation with gambling, sex, or creativity often comes unexpectedly. Thankfully, my husband's brain chose creativity. So, as if composing music on his computer was not enough, he began to create sculptures from palm tree materials plentiful in our neighborhood. He made birds and reindeer and fish and lizards out of palm fronds and bark. After a session in his shop, he'd come in, covered in shavings, paint and glue, take his meds, and flop out for an hour or two.

Meanwhile, I'd eked out a few more lines of poetry or a paragraph or two.

Being apart for a while each day, claiming our own mental space, proved to be one way we made it through the long haul.

But we also had rituals of being together. Rituals provide comfort, a feeling of security. We ate all our meals together, with a spoken grace beforehand. Whatever we were doing separately, we stopped at 5:30 to have a drink and watch the evening news. And we always kissed goodnight.

One charming and sustaining ritual was family night, instituted by our local son. Every Tuesday evening, we ate together and watched a movie. At first we went to a restaurant; later, our son brought carry-out. These nights were very important to us—they kept us connected to our son and his family, they gave us something to look forward to, and later to reminisce about and share.

This ritual was part of our decision to try our best to maintain social contacts. For years after he was diagnosed, we were able to attend concerts and plays and art exhibits. On nights when we were going out, we varied the timing of his medications to give him optimum benefit for the occasions.

Jan Seale

We attended church regularly, with his own personal niche in the pews for his wheelchair. His place was in a side aisle, the same aisle people used returning to their seats after communion. Now my husband had a fairly private personality, with a large personal space around him. In his public career as professor and orchestral conductor, he was well liked but there was always respect maintained for this invisible moat around him. After he became wheelchair-enabled, and was sitting on the aisle used by commun-icants returning to their seats, people began to touch him as they passed by--on the hand, arm, or shoulder, always very lightly and lovingly, but boldly and deliberately. They seemed to have a non-verbal kindness they wanted to express to him. And he came to relish this extra blessing. People with Parkinson's can soften, grow more tolerant, be more grateful, gain perspective. There are few enough enhancements in life with Parkinson's.

My sons and I were in a brave new world in dealing with a Parkinsonian father and husband. I will never forget the night I had to call our local son and his partner to come across town and get Carl up from a fall he had taken. When we finally wrestled him back to bed, Erren leaned over him and said, "That's all for you, sailor! Sleep it off!" We all broke out laughing.

When Carl and I married, I thought Carl hung the moon. Years later, I had to hang my own moon and help him hang his.

And just as time took Carl into an ever-evolving condition of disability, I was called upon to remember that I as a caregiver was changing as well.

I love what a great American writer, Somerset Maugham, wrote about this:

> We are not the same
> persons this year as last:
> nor are those we love. It is
> a happy chance if we,
> changing, continue to love
> a changed person.

As a caregiver, I felt the benign neglect of not getting as much appreciation as I deserved or could use. There were times when I had to be my own best friend. One day when I was feeling extra sorry for myself, I ran across a quote on a calendar that startled me out of my moping. It asked, "Is it so important that those in your life fully appreciate how much you mean to them? Or can you get along just fine knowing it for yourself?"

Sometimes I felt really desperate. I learned to think of immediate solutions—practical things like calling the doctor, or visiting a medical supply store, or looking up a problem online. With distraction, I might settle down, understand that feelings pass but I had a code, a standard of belief in what I was doing. It meant that I might think of myself as the chairman of my committee, and tell my tired, frustrated self that on any given day I didn't get but one vote.

Carl and I were very fortunate in that we both had a crazy sense of humor. I recommend using humor any time it works. Funny things act as powerful antidotes. They break tension. They put our troubles in perspective. Laughing together is so healing. Carl and I had a set of silly names for certain things. His name for Parkinson's Disease was Sparkie and for himself, Parkie. He christened his walker "Rolanda." If he occasionally lost her, we would go through the house calling "Rolanda, where are you?"

When he graduated from the walker to his power wheelchair, we dubbed it "the electric chair." Our big white plain retrofitted van we called "the bread truck."

We had certain ongoing jokes. One afternoon we had a particularly unsatisfactory visit with a member of the medical profession who had been recommended to us. We simply were not on the same wave length with this person. We were barely out the door of his office when we began to snigger. Crossing the parking lot, Carl said, "What we need...are some cheese enchiladas." Sometimes comfort food is great medicine.

Caregivers worldwide must have an If-I-had-it-to-do-all-over-again compartment. It's not possible to be a human and not make some mistakes— especially when you're exhausted and your patience, reasoning, and logic have gone off-duty.

If I had it to do all over again, I'd be more mindful of the ergonomics of Parkinson's. For example, we had our little war over the position of his plate at the table. He seemed to push it out, away from him, as he ate. Two or three times during the meal, I would reach over and push it back directly in front of him. Otherwise, there would be spilled food on the table. He never said a word to me but seemed resentful of my helpfulness. It was only after he was gone, that the light bulb went off in my head. His arms didn't bend well enough to have his plate directly in front of him. It was easier for him to scoop up his food a few inches away from the edge of the table.

If I had it to do over, I'd try to be more observant about Carl's mental state. He was quiet and stoical by nature, so when his responses were off, I chalked it up to tiredness or age. That was *my* illusion. All along he was struggling with reasoning and memory, but I thought it was his personality.

A story will show you what I mean. The last couple of years of Carl's life, he developed a serious low blood pressure problem. He had orthostatic hypotension; when he stood, he fainted within seconds. At first it was occasional, then more frequent, and finally, inevitable. A typical event: he would roll into his study in his wheel chair, see a book he wanted from a high shelf, and stand up to get it. Book in hand, he would faint. I would hear a noise, go to him, and find him on the floor. This happened over and over.

His doctors warned him not to stand when he was alone. We all warned him not to stand. Still, he kept standing up when he was alone.

Caregivers are fixers, and the trait serves us well most of the time. I was going to fix this. First, I got a doorbell set. He wore the push-button on a terry cloth wrist bracelet and I wore the chimer on my belt. When he needed to stand up, or needed me for anything else, he was to push the button on his wrist, which would alert me to come to his aid. In other words, he would ring my chimes!

This worked about 75% of the time. The other 25%, he said he just forgot. I suspected he was exercising his strong sense of independence, which I had seen manifested over a long marriage. Either that, or he truly did not want to bother me. Still, I gave him a little lecture about "forgetting."

Then things got darker. One night he "forgot," stood, fainted, fell against his book case, and nearly tore his ear lobe off. After an all-nighter in the emergency room—on the way home I told him that this was a heck of a way to mimic the artist Van Gogh—with his bandage over his ear. Home and in a more serious tone, I said that he *had* to call me before he stood up, and I extracted a promise from him that he would.

Next I tried tying two soft scarves together and loosely tethering him to his wheelchair. I told him they were just to remind him, when he started to rise, to call me. I was glad to come help him with whatever he was wanting, but he had to call me; did he understand, blah, blah, blah?

I went to the other side of the house.

In a while, he rang my chimes. Ah-hah! I thought. Finally something's working. When I reached him, he said, "Why are these silly scarves around me? Don't you know I've got to stand up!"

The light finally dawned. I'd been operating on the assumption that he was still the orchestra conductor...that those brainy traits which made him a fine leader, a college professor, a reasoning husband and father were all intact. After all, he still conversed, ate, even worked hours on end at his computer. To be ailing in the body was one thing; to be changing mentally and behaviorally—these were harder for me to grasp.

When I surrendered to the notion that he had a well-concealed loss of short-term memory, the fight about standing up became an instant non-issue. The truth was: He simply did not remember his history of falling. The consequences of standing up were inconsequential to him. The solution was clear: It was time to hire a person to sit in the room with him.

At times, it was hard for me as a caregiver to count my blessings, but over the long haul there were some. Who among us would not accept gifts to our personalities?

I became more determined, practical, and knowledgeable. There was hard-won humility and understanding. And I hope along the way I increased in patience, kindness, forgiveness. For me, there was a physical strength I didn't know I was capable of.

I can't say I was happier, but I became a deeper person. I don't say this for an effect of haughtiness but I came to look on others who seemed not to have a care in the world as people who hadn't gotten the benefit of a full range of feelings. Simply put, I had swum in a deeper ocean.

I look back on my twenty years of being an active caregiver of a person suffering from an incurable disease and wonder that my life took such a turn. It's been said that our only response to being allowed to live is gratefulness. For me, that includes being grateful that I was able to share my life with another who needed me and whom I loved.

Caregivers are in the front seat of the rollercoaster ride of Parkinson's. We may lose our lunch, scream in terror, or laugh hysterically, but above all, we hold on. Such a ride!

IV. Groundings

Limes, Anyone?
2009

The other day we looked out our front windows and saw a neighbor under one of our Mexican lime trees, shaking away. My husband went out. "Caught you!" he said, laughing. And the man, who has gleaning rights, agreed. Seems he needed a few of the spiky little fruits to prepare his tilapia for guests that night.

It's harvest time again. Our two front-yard Mexican lime trees are groaning under the weight of their fruit. Every year in July, we experience a virtual wave of neighborly love. Morning and evening walkers stop by, presumably just to chat. But their eyes travel upward. They lick their lips as they remark how large and healthy our trees are.

Yesterday we asked our yard crew to trim one branch that was threatening the roof of our carport. A little while passed and the doorbell rang. Could the worker have a sack please? The branch was loaded with new limes. He'd pick them off and give them to us—and, uh—if we didn't want them, he'd be glad to take them off our hands.

For several years we have enhanced the good will of our local friends and even our long-distance relatives by means of these little green edible golf balls. Mexican, or Key lime differs from the larger Persian lime, with its thick skin and dumbed-down flavor. Loaded with all manner of nutritious elements—polyphenols, antioxidants, fiber—Mexican limes not only give a health benefit but pack a wallop of eye-squinching sour flavor that complements scores of dishes.

My husband bought these two trees as saplings on the side of the road about ten years ago and planted them in our front yard. He continues his paternalistic attitude toward them as they dominate the entire area. During the fruiting seasons—twice a year—he goes at least once a day like Little Red Riding Hood with his basket to pick up the ripe ones that fall to the ground.

In the kitchen, his farmer's pride evaporates. I am allowed to sort, wash, squeeze, freeze, and prepare dishes with them. Sometimes we think we have exhausted uses for them, and then we find another. The obvious ones get a heavy workout at our house. At high season, friends entering the house are bold to inquire, "Got any of that limeade you make?" I have to admit, through the years I've developed a cravenly delicious formula: 1 cup fresh squeezed lime juice dissolving 3 cups sugar (not a misprint), then 3 quarts of water. If I have it, a crushed sprig of mint goes into the pitcher.

For some reason, lime juice makes almost any dish taste better. It is the ultimate flavor enhancer. We squeeze it into soups, use it in salad dressing and salsas, and garnish papaya, avocado, watermelon, and banana. Okay, it makes these a bit mushy if you don't eat them right away.

That's because lime juice is the ultimate tenderizer. Give chicken or tuna an hour under this mesmerizing liquid and the result could make you famous.

And after all the edible uses, lime juice can be used to wash vegetables, gargle, doctor mosquito bites, cure toe fungus, and rinse hair.

We here in South Texas are the willing recipients of many things we have nothing to do with procuring. Mexican limes love us because of our alkaline soil, having come across the world from Southeast Asia. These tart little orbs got handed off to the North Africans and near Easterners by Arab traders. Somewhere along the way—probably at a common proselytizing meal—Crusaders took them to Palestine and Mediterranean Europe. By 1250, they were being grown in Italy and France.

Then dear old Columbus did something right: limes are listed on the bill of lading for his second voyage in 1493 to the New World. Easily grown from the seeds of the fruit, the trees were introduced into the subtropical United States and Central America.

We here on the border naturally call them Mexican limes, rather than favoring the name given by our domestic citrus rival, the Florida Keys. Our only concession seems to be in the name Key Lime Pie.

July and August are lime-dominant months at our house. We gather a couple of thousand limes during that period. Another 500 or so come off in the second season, around Christmas. And what on earth do two city dwellers do with all these limes? It's not as though we could eat them like mashed potatoes.

We give away as many as friendship allows. Several of our neighbors, as already indicated, are heads-up for our sharing. Others have their own lime trees, and this fact we have to keep mutually telling each other year after year.

And then there are the squeeze evenings. At some desperate point, the fridge is full of limes, gathered at a half bushel a day, and we have to "work them up," as my farming grandmothers would say.

We are on our second juicer, the first one's notched spindle worn down by thousands of acidic sacrifices. My husband mans the knife and cutting board and I stand over the machine, making a game of how fast I can place the lime half on the rotating spindle. The juice sluices out, most of the seeds caught in the holding collar. After a while, I notice I have a full pitcher and must transfer the three cups to a larger container. Eventually, I re-strain, for hardy seeds that have slipped through, and measure the juice into one-cup portions in small jars for the freezer. I know, I know, you recom-mend plastic bags, but these often leak, and besides, "canning" with Ball jars makes me feel ancestral and virtuous.

What I do not like is the clean-up. One may think Mexican lime juice is so sour it couldn't possibly be sticky, but it is--syrupy, ticky-tacky, filled-with-sugar sticky.

Regardless of how careful we are, the hapless little things exact their own revenge. As we work at detonation, the juice squirts and sprays. Eventually, it drips off to the floor. We make the trip to the compost with the heavy bucket of rinds—bless their little dessicated hearts—and it's back into the house to purge the counters, mop the floor, clean our glasses, and take a shower.

As I write this, I figure I have about one more week of peace before the evening juicing ritual starts. We are already heading out with gift bags of limes to hairdresser, minister, masseur, library clerk, and exercise partners. And a few are already gently refusing them, or taking them to give to their neighbors and friends. It's a spreading epidemic.

Soon we will hang a sack on the mailbox for Oscar, our mailman. A couple of trips north will find us traveling with loaded picnic iceboxes of limes to grace our way into the hearts of relatives.

Some lime-tree owners—and there are many in our area—do not collect their limes. The ground beneath their trees is a sea of decaying yellow. I envy their lack of concern, their profligacy. My rural ancestral past does not allow me such liberties. Whatever grows and is edible, I have to harvest. (Just now, the bananas and papayas on our backyard trees are coming ripe, without any particular care except water. We have our South Texas version of a Victory Garden. And maybe we're going to need it.)

Today the limes hang quietly in the bright sunshine of our yard, in silent nanoseconds growing larger, juicier, sweeter, more sour. They're not much prone to pests—though one year chinch bugs sneaked in to initial each fruit with a little blip. Grackles tend to borrow a few for use oiling their feathers and wasps have a penchant for making black dots on their surface. Still, the season is here and there's more than enough for us and all our wildlife.

Something besides the utility of the limes keeps beckoning us to them. Is it just greed for the abundant and luscious?

In them, nature calls out far beyond our needs. They are like the stars, or grains of sand, in their overabundance. Their excessive giving is flabbergasting. They answer our need for astonishment, for admiring what is out of control. We harvest them and know the most elemental of human activities, taking the bounty of the earth.

And they put us into a community of believers. "Oh my gosh!" say our visitors, looking up into the trees and pointing. We smile and step back into the kitchen to get a bag for them. It's Christmas in July.

Reading the Obits

I have long wondered why I read the obituaries every day. I used to think it was so I could keep up with acquaintances in the community, people not exactly friends but not strangers either. I have a horror of meeting such a person in the grocery store, inquiring about the spouse and being embar-rassed when they say, "You didn't know? Pat died in February." But I think that is not the main reason I read the obituaries.

The real one is that in these obituaries—I'm never sure who writes them—there's a kind of ultimate poetry of the world. I like the euphemisms that the family, or someone designated at the funeral home or the news-paper, uses. They seldom write that so-and-so simply died or succumbed to old age. The people who die in my hometown paper do soft poetic things like "enter into eternal rest" or "pass on to a better life."

Atheists and Presbyterians "complete their journey on earth." Sometimes people become angels on a certain day, say, at 4:30 on a Wednes-day afternoon. Baptists often "go into the presence of their Precious Lord and Savior," occasionally sitting on Jesus' lap or flying into the Lord's loving arms.

Often there'll be a sentence that makes me whoop. Take "Mom died kicking and screaming, that is—being her ordinary self." Or, "Carlos loved his dog more than his friends." One account reported that the departed "loved shooting white doves, Canadian geese, and pheasants." Another reported that "his beloved wife served him cheesecake on their 55th wedding anniversary."

Typos may lend a certain poetic license to the notices. Services for a woman will be at Our Lady, Queen of Angles Church. A venerable soldier was a member of "the U.S. Calvary" at Ft. Ringgold. Reports of the body's "internment" are more often the case than their interment. And the enablement of the dead person to reconstitute is pretty astounding, as in "she will be having her visitation today at 5 p.m."

I like the way their faces shine out of the type, the smile on most of them belying the fact that this pose will be their obituary picture. How would they have posed had they only known? Roberto's shadow mimics him on the white background like a death twin. Maria Esther's neck is missing, smothered in a frilly white blouse. Manny's head is tilted back, revealing the snake tattoo on his neck. Jose Luis wears his best white ten gallon and Genoveva, ever the party girl, has a telltale hand resting on her left shoulder.

Sometimes there's a "before" and "after," wizened faces of nonagenarians matched to their handsome World War II soldier or bridal visages.

And I can never get enough of the romantic multisyllabic names in the obituary section here in South Texas. There's Comodela, Juvenal, Exequio, Ethelvina, Policarpio, and Demencio. There's Gumecindo, Eulogia, Hidolina. Short of going down to the courthouse and asking to read the tax rolls, we find here a great perk for living outside the dull Anglo mainstream culture.

If the town folk have not cooperated by dying in sufficient numbers, the space on the obit page may be filled with appropriate ads. Once, right next to the account of a dear departed soul, there was a hurricane preparedness article, where we were to go online and "Roll over to get started." Another ad, way up close and personal, admonished us to "Hurry before this offer expires."

Today is Good Friday and I've had a good one. A friend came and stayed for lunch on the porch. The strong coffee we drank to the accompaniment of leftover plum cake has given me the zing I needed to love life even more fervently for a while this afternoon. I told Al this had been a Good Friday, because he came. He demurred, joking that he hoped his visit did not cause the degree of suffering of that of the first Good Friday. We agreed that it had not.

But just for sure, I'll check out the obits tomorrow. My picture better not be there.

Some of My Best Friends are Rocks

Outside my study window are six thousand pounds of rocks. This might not seem remarkable to a Vermonter or someone living on a Rocky Mountain high, but for a resident of the flat alluvial plain of South Texas, it speaks to a differentness.

When we decided to xeriscape our yard sixteen years ago, the first thing to go was the grass. No more little boys in residence to tumble on it; no more need for smooth greenness; no more will power to change the sprinkler every thirty minutes on watering days.

The day they brought the rocks, our neighbors gathered safely on the opposite side of the street to watch the dump truck. One smiled wanly and cracked, "Goin' Arizona on us, are ya'?"

Then a remarkable thing happened. Several workmen gathered with shovels and rakes and began to spread out the millennia of the ages. This gravel was not the gritty stuff that gets lodged in tire grooves and goes tack-tack-tack when cars slow at intersections. No, the good-sized rocks—knobs, eggs, doll-house ottomans, peach pits, erasers—contained an astonishing variety of transplanted geology.

Today I have gone out my front door, stooped down in the drizzling rain, and gathered in five minutes several thousand years of geological history. There's lumpy igneous formed from the molten rock of volcanoes, varying in appearance from a tiger's caramel striped coat to a purplish flinty arrowhead. Sedimentary stones, with their chalk, lime, calcium, and sand form a bridge between mineral and animal. Moments ago I gathered a stone which, by all appearances, began as a piece of coral, then rolled and tumbled through the Texas Mesozoic sea until now it resembles the brain of a small animal. As for metamorphic rock, I hold in my hand a heavy, egg-shaped stone, unremarkably brown but on closer inspection, displaying thin bands of white through and through, a certain indication that this rock has been subjected to various periods of stress, sort of a geological hiccup.

One year, a spate of school boys walked home afternoons past my house. They could not keep their hands off the rocks, filling their pockets and pounding each other as they loped off down the street. I had to lie in wait for them several afternoons until my scolding broke them of the habit. The thing was, I couldn't half blame them, the rocks being so inviting.

As a child I could not resist picking up pretty rocks. What child does, as a wondering young spirit? Now I have my own rock-finding playground. I can go out early in the morning and survey my treasure. The colors are spot-on: burnt orange, glistening black, soft grays and browns, butter and honey, touches of mauve. When I bend over, intending to pick up a lime or get the morning paper, I may not be able to resist picking up a rock for my collection. The whole yard lies as a bed of history—transplanted rocks of ages.

It may be a coal-black lump threaded through with pristine white lines, a heavy sharp-edged flint with a hint of tool or arrow, a peculiar yellowish stubby cigar that has tumbled ages in a riverbed. It could be smooth as a baby's belly, or—too sensitive for the ride—crushed/halved jaggedly. Gray mushrooms, white doughy maidens, stones inscribed with the language of snails. These go first in my robe pocket, then to the collection that sits near the porch. I'll look at them as I pass in and out, on my way to the ephemera of the day. My glance will steady me, remind me of things that were here long before me, will be here long after I am gone.

A rock is the mysterious gift of the earth, all kinds of them formed basically at one stage or another from chipping, sloughing, burning, dropping, cracking, melting, dividing from the soil of the stars of which our earth was forged.

My whole life I have been possessed with the notion that everything is living. Everything. This includes the rocks in my yard. So as I collect them, I must suffer through naming them, offering sympathy, compliments, inquiring about their origins.

How do they lie in my yard—with pleasure? uneasily? longing for home?

My neighbor came over last week and brought his grandchild. While he and I talked, this bright five year old marched around the yard gathering rocks. He lined up a dozen or so on the walkway that he thought had some similarity and then he and his grandfather went home. Of course, the line of rocks is still there, just like Bobby placed them, and will be for a long time.

In the morning, I may find a stone or two has leapt the bounds of the yard and is staging a solo appearance on the driveway. Who or what placed it there in the night?

146

Many years ago, a plumber put our children onto the path of rock appreciation. He came to our house out in the country to do some plumbing work, and observing three young boys, he asked them if they'd like a rock tumbling kit. "Sure," they said, not having the slightest notion what he was talking about. The next time he came, he brought a lidded canister, a rotating platform for it to rest on, some polishing grit and a sack of rather unremarkable small rocks. He showed them how to place the rocks, the grit, and a little water in the canister, balance it on the rotating platform, and plug in the motor—all in a little tool shed out back (because tumbling rocks make quite a noise). They were politely interested.

We let it run for about two weeks, then opened it up. Voila! Beautiful smooth brightly-colored gemstones—tiger eyes, creamy opals, dazzling purple crystals—all ready for a boy's pocket or for a jewelry setting. That plumber has been dead for many years but I still have a small rock pendant in my jewelry box from that period of activity to remind me how passionate that plumber was about rocks, and how he taught our boys the magic of making treasure out of dross with the rock tumbling kit.

Stones are not sky, plant, or animal but something of great spirit conjuring up a definition of *being,* saying how matter matters. They are dirt on steroids.

Receiving

I'm standing in line, leaning a little on the long counter/barrier where people puzzle over money orders or rest heavy packages and postal machines.

I'm thinking how the post office in our border town is more modern than the rest of the nation probably presumes. Popular too. Even with five customer stations, there's always a queue.

Off to one side, a blue door labeled "Passports" opens and closes constantly with worried-looking people entering or leaving. Sometimes a uniformed man waddles out, impeded by pepper spray and a stun gun, and leaves importantly through the automated main doors.

But now a rooster crows. This is not a good omen. I have just read about a schizophrenic who acted on voices she heard.

There it is again, a good strong cock-a-doodle-do. No one moves. Maybe it doesn't translate well into Spanish...Not!

I size up my closest queue mate, a young woman in leather wristbands and gladiator sandals. "Excuse me. Did you hear a rooster crow?" I ask.

She jiggles one leg. "It was just somebody's ringtone," she says not unkindly, suddenly fascinated by a poster explaining the difference in priority and first class.

"Cock-a-doodle-do!" Again. Avian-speak amidst florescent lights and government issue linoleum.

And so, the rhythm continues: the line moves up, the rooster crows. But now each time, it comes from a different location behind the ubiquitous gray privacy wall.

I have time to think up a profane little story where it's Chanticleer himself who crows three times before poor old mixed-up Peter denies Christ. Yes, it is probably schizophrenia.

Then I remember a curious penned yard on the road to Bluetown, a little community just a stone's throw from the Rio Grande. A dozen tiny pitched-roof doll houses sit strategically apart, with a lone rooster staked outside each. Hmmm, I remember thinking. Hmmm, such bravado.

It's my turn at the counter. "How can I help you?" the pleasant postal lady asks. (She knows she is being recorded; being timed; she is up for a performance review.)

I ask for a roll of stamps and while she's getting my change, there's that sound again, from a different location.

"Excuse me, but is that a rooster I hear, maybe more than one?" I ask.

She smiles. "It's just one this time. He doesn't like it in 'will call' so they're moving him around, trying to get him to quiet down."

Somebody *mailed* a rooster?"

"We've called the addressee. The man said he'd come for him soon." She glances at the wall clock. "It's been four hours." Her eyes flush red.

She quickly counts my change. "We had ten in here last week. A regular barnyard. Have a nice day. Next, please."

Vegetable Hope

My xeriscaped yard has no grass. Still, it is a verdant cornucopia of astounding fierce and delicate co-existing beings, things as alive as we are.

On any given morning, I try to immediately connect with my yard. I open the kitchen blind and survey the small area outside. Has anything happened to the world—my world—in the night? Have the mesquites showered the patio with their minute slivers of foliage? Has a cat upset a pot? Are the ants out—those pesky cutter ants—the snake in my Eden? A kiskadee is doing acrobatics on the main electrical line. He is jumping, swinging, calling "kisk-a-dee—Here I be"—his bright yellow breast catching the first sun. A hummingbird frantically plunges into the red blossoms of the fire spike.

The night-blooming cereus is extravagantly ornate in its saucer-sized blooms, reminding me of the spinthrift unecological nature of nature. Moss on the slabs of the fountain gives off its soft fuzzy message. The red sexy pendulous blossom of the banana plant swings above, inciting the bees that feed off the tiny inner blooms, each one of which, after many months, will transform itself into a fragrant edible piece of fruit.

The papaya trees number eight now. Last year there were 30, many of which had planted themselves with the help of birds all around the perimeter. Now there are seven females and one male. The gardener and I saw to that ratio. It's like in animal husbandry—most farms need only one male specie to take care of the harem. Antithetical to our human notions of sexuality, the papaya males have delicate lacy blooms on long extended stems, the females sturdy tulip-like blossoms close to the trunk. The fruit of the mama papayas sits on the stalk day after day, months going by, only growing greener and a little bigger. Then one day I notice a certain apricot blush on a lower fruit of the stack. I'll have to check it every morning. If I miss a day, a golden crowned woodpecker or possum will beat me to it.

In the front yard I go to pay particular attention to the two *agaves americanas*. They have individually stretched themselves over six feet of ground and risen ten feet into the air. Some people call them century plants but they don't last any longer than about 30 years. I have already lost three.

They took a while to die, and gave out signals in advance, a slowly rising 30-ft. high stalk laden with yellow flowers. When the stalks rise up out of the base, there is nothing to be done to prevent the eventual death of the plant. Cutting off the stalk won't help. It's a rare combination of circum-stances: blooms herald death. One of the stalks was so heavy it pulled over the entire plant, plopping down on my neighbor's trimmed St. Augustine grass. I went out with hacksaw and determination to remove the stem before it could do more damage. It promptly showed me who was boss. I could no more saw the large stalk with its circumference of 12 inches than I could lift it to drag to the alley. It was no different from a good-sized tree up beside my efforts.

But now I go about inspecting one of the two remaining ones. A month ago I noticed that the older had began to suffer badly, but not from the appearance of a death stalk. Its broad lower leaves—long, heavy, with thorns lining the edges and a grim needle spike punctuating the end—drooped unnaturally. Brown juice oozed from their base. When I gripped one with both hands, carefully avoiding the thorns and spike, it came loose from the trunk and sent me staggering backward, grappling for footage. Then I saw the problem: thousands of ants disturbed by my invasion. They may have been angry at the moment. But just before, they were no doubt happy, very happy, since they were supping on mescal, the sweet alcoholic material of the agave. I removed the other ailing limbs and doctored the plant all around with granules. Today it seems to be holding its own.

Sometimes I wonder why I have it in my yard. It takes up a great deal of space and every so often, I have to snip off each dagger-like spike so that my visiting grandchildren will not blind themselves. Still, it's the thing visitors point to: "How old is that thing?" "Is that what they make tequila with?" (No, that's another variety) "Where did you get it?"

I like to remember the legacy of my agave in the family's past. My late husband, suffering from Parkinson's but still on his feet and eager to be busy, took some of the giant blade-like spears and spent several hours stripping them into tough strands of fiber. When he had a generous amount, he wound them in a loose ball and shipped them in a box to our daughter-in-law. She in turn wove them into one of the tapestries she was fashioning. All in the family, this plant.

At Christmastime, when the agave was a youngster, I could attach shiny balls to its limbs for a nice effect. It long ago outgrew that possibility.

Now I take down from the storeroom a multicolored disc and attach it to a strong spotlight. It is known in the family as Pappaw's Light and has given various moving shades of color to front yard objects over decades. This contraption goes to a place near the agave where I spend a while getting it balanced, then return to the house to switch it on.

Voila! My imposing stark giant of desert nature is transformed with softly undulating waves of pink, lavender, and green. It's an instant Christmas tree, giving delight to my neighbors and passersby. I sigh. It's a plant for all seasons, and I'll love, yes love it through its months-long slow anomalous death by flowering.

For now, there's the testimony of plants and humans coexisting. There's the season of lights, beginning again, the planting of hope and the promise of one more year of my yard waiting for me every sunrise.

Sparrow-watching

A group of birders-by-marriage was congregated to wait out the return of their birding spouses at a retreat center in the hill country of Texas. Talk went somewhat unnaturally to the subject of birds, and especially why these folks resisted becoming birders along with their husbands and wives. One man explained that his favorite birds were sparrows, but only because he could actually *see* them and note what they were.

During that same event, the birding expert leading the group allowed as how sparrows were the best practice for beginning birders. She said, "Beginning birders are apt to see more exotic birds than are really there. But sparrows are always there."

One of my earliest remembrances of these little brown-flaked birds is, I am ashamed to say, the object of a very dear lesson. Having no sons, my father gambled on the hunter instinct in my sister and me by making slingshots for us. These were sturdy "Y's" with retractable strips of inner tube material which we loaded with small pebbles and aimed at various declared targets.

Everything was going fine until one of us actually hit a bird in the bush. Mortified, we rushed to see if it was dead. No, but the sparrow (was it a lark, a black-throated, a white-crowned, a chipping, a Baird's, a Cassin's?) was looking mighty sick. Filled with remorse that our aim had actually been true, we rushed the little thing into the house and made a shoe box hospital for it. As I recall, supplicant though we were, the bird expired.

As retribution, from that time on, I have been condemned to waste a good deal of time watching sparrows. I try to remember that Jesus himself spoke up for the sparrows, proclaiming that no less a being than God noticed when a sparrow fell to the ground. So then of course God noticed when my sister and I murdered a sparrow.

In our area of South Texas, sparrows have about as much status with non-birders as grackles and hackberry trees. That is to say, we generally don't think much about them. They're brown or gray; they're speckled or splotched; they're small, they hop, they cheep. The modifier "only" is often coupled with their name, as in "It was only a sparrow."

Yet, local birders and those coming from all over the world have identified 25 different kinds of sparrows here in the Lower Rio Grande Valley of Texas. One, the olive sparrow, which is only found in South Texas, became a world-class star recently when it was spotted in the brush and the news went out on the birding hotline, drawing birders from Canada, Europe, Japan and New Zealand to fly in, behold it and chalk one up on their life lists.

Sparrows happen to be the champion number-setters for wild birds. And they are rather interesting to watch, if you don't mind lingering a while with the little fellows. A flock lives in my back yard and I'd swear they have a telegraph system when I put out a few crumbs or seeds. It's barely a minute until they're coming from various directions to feed. When I step out while they're feeding, they swoop away in perfect synchrony, the flutter of their collective wings making a sound like so many tongues clicking.

And speaking of tongues, these seed eaters possess an extra bone in their tongues. (Who knew to begin with that tongues had bones?) Sparrow tongue bones are said to help prop up the tongue while anchoring seeds in their mouths.

It seems sparrows would rather fight than eat. When they are grazing, they fitfully defend their patch against perceived intruders with paranoid rushes and pecks.

And what is going on when they land in a bush all together and begin cheeping loudly, making the bush jiggle and sway? Even my sons as lads noticed the phenomenon and adopted a call to arms, "Sparrow fight! Sparrow fight!" which they eventually extended to any of their friends they felt were beginning a ludicrous quarrel.

In the past, it seems all small birds were called sparrows. Now the towhees and finches and buntings have their own avian slots, and what we know as sparrows can live on in their cheeping ubiquitous millions. Common? Yes, of course. But as Amitendra Nath Tagore observed, "The sparrow is sorry for the peacock at the burden of its tail."

Sparrows make it easy for us all to be bird watchers.

Falling Leaves, Rising Spirits

I deplane at Baltimore/Washington International on Thursday, Oct. 17, 2002 and everything feels normal. It's properly crowded. Am I headed right toward Baggage? I hope my ride is waiting for me, inside.

I'm here in Sniperland to lead a workshop on women's wisdom. There's a dark humor in the wisdom (lack?) of this woman flying *into* Montgomery County, Maryland.

It started one day two weeks before when the organizer and I were on the phone. "Wait a minute," Brenda says, "I've got to put you on hold." When she returns, she says, "With the news I just received, you may not want to come up this way. There's a crazy sharpshooter loose."

Oh, yeah?" the adventuresome me replies. "Well, they'll catch him in a day or two."

But they haven't, and I've come, I tell my heroine persona, because I'm standing up with those who refuse to cancel their lives for the agenda of terrorists.

My more honest self reminds me that I'm under contract, and they've assured me they're not canceling the retreat. And my devious nature-loving self is trying again to see an autumn leaf show, after having to cancel last year's post-9/11 "leaf peepers" tour to New England.

You might say I'm autumn-challenged. Growing up in a little town in north Texas, I dived into crisp pyramids of raked oak and maple leaves in a rare permissible display of abandon. Much later, dry leaves followed me into sympathetic sorrow. Our son left his hamster's cage door open and the tabby helped herself. Lying on the floor disconsolate, the eight year old raised his head long enough to say, "I wish I was a dead leaf. That way I would drop off the tree. But also someone would step on me and crush me."

In the fall on the Tex-Mex border, we have "bird herds" viewing migrations rather than "leaf peepers." Here October brings an almost singular seasonal tree display. Jillions of tiny yellow stars appear on our streets and lawns, heralding the maturation of the golden rain tree, an exotic that made its way into the southern tip of Texas and couldn't get enough of our mild climate and delta-rich soil.

By mid-October the plenteous trees are laden with small yellow origami boxes. Inside are the seeds for the lacey saplings that will dot our flower beds in spring. But first, the clusters of little boxes slowly turn to a rich coral orange, then to dusty rose, lingering a while as the mascot of our official autumn.

Now, walking with the throngs of passengers down the terminal hallway, I remember guiltily that I haven't told my 91-year-old mother I'm coming. I have to forego her prayers in deference to her painful worry.

Brenda is there for me at the door, and after we greet each other, we wait in the parking garage for the elevator. The minutes seem like hours. Brenda says it's best to keep moving, just slightly, in a little drunken dance, to keep from being a possible cross-hairs target. How marvelous is human adaptation. "It's not the same magnitude, of course," Brenda opines, "but it feels inside the way Nine-Eleven felt."

Out on the beltway, she announces, "I've got one little delivery to make on our way. It won't take but five minutes."

I swallow my bravura. "Do I have to stay in the car?"

No. You go in with me."

I'd never thought too much about how early it gets dark in the Northeast. I notice police cars sitting in the median. Large blue tarps cover the fronts of gas stations. People have been picked off by the sniper while they fueled their cars.

The lights are bright around the church. Brenda pulls in, cuts the motor, and we freeze in place. A white van screams its presence nearby—we have been told that might be the suspect's transportation. Then we relax: workers are loading the van after a blood drive.

Now our steps are springy...even sprinty. Inside, a surprise—fifty voices rehearsing Christmas music. I search their faces for stress. All I hear is grand singing. Whatever the worries, they're checked at the door.

The next day we start out early for the retreat center outside Hagerstown. First we'll take a jaunt up to Pennsylvania to visit the battle-field at Gettysburg, a treat my hosts have promised. (The native Texan in me marvels that we can take a side trip to another state, do some sight-seeing, and be back well before supper.)

The granite markers sit solemnly testifying to the bravery of Robertson's Brigade or Reade's Offensive or Longstreet's Artillery. We stand on a gentle bluff overlooking what they tell me was the bloodiest fray of all. Today it's a meadow resplendent in late summer grass, surrounded by colorful fall woods. Far off, a dignified General Lee reigns in his wooded surrounds. I make myself still and small, try to comprehend that in the midst of this loveliness, 51,000 men died in three days.

*The woods are lovely, dark, and deep...*back at the Mt. Aetna Retreat Center. We settle into our dorm for an inky black sleep, far from the Beltway Booger. But the next day, and the next, we don't linger in the woods, nor seek out the Appalachian Trailhead only a mile away. Especially we don't after we hear a rifle discharging repeatedly even though it's followed by the reassuring yelps of hounds.

On the last afternoon, after we've pledged ourselves to be true to our womanly gifts, I go into a little grove of trees near our meeting place and pick up leaves, lipstick red maples and mustard yellow oak. I filch a few long-stemmed Virginia creepers ablaze on a tree trunk. Soon my new Maryland friends, autumn-proud, join me, donating handfuls of pretties to my sack. (My salvaged leaves make it home in a plastic bag, ready to be preserved between sheets of wax paper until I can share with my grandchildren their shouting colors and traceable shapes.)

We go to bed happy on Saturday night. All has been calm, all bright since Thursday. Yet we awaken to the news that a traveler has been gunned down at a restaurant while we gazed into last night's fire, told stories, and bonded.

Sunday afternoon back in Gaithersburg, we drag our camp trappings hurriedly through glittering sunlight into our host's townhouse. No one comments, no one jokes. We just get inside.

Monday, it's necessary to do a few things on our way to the airport. We need to go to a store in a mall. "Hmm," says Beth, my ride this time. She's been about to park beside a white van with a rack on top. She circles around. "Get out here and go in that door and wait for me," she orders, pulling up to the curb. I hurry, walking the prescribed zigzag. Inside, the mall is nearly empty, shop clerks standing with folded arms in their doorways.

On the plane, high over the Mississippi, I draw from my purse the plastic bag full of fall leaves. Maybe it's the altitude but I'm looking at their beauty like I'd never seen a fall leaf before, like I'd never cut one out of orange or red construction paper and stuck it to the window of my second-grade classroom long ago in Texas.

I can't figure out beauty and death so close together. They don't hold still in my head right. All that seems stable are the set mouths, some even smiling, and the vigilant eyes of those I'm flying away from, good American people doing the best they can. They are literally willing their lives—to hold a retreat, to get groceries and gas, to shelter their children up the school walkways, to begin rehearsing Christmas music. They could be Bosnians or Syrians or Civil War soldiers. They'll have another four days before their nightmare is over.

I come home and what greets me? News of the death of my neighbor. And what's in his yard? The boxy coral fall blooms of the golden rain tree, shouting out "Life again next year!" as clearly as the red and yellow leaves I unpack.

How Child Got to Be Himself on the Rio Grande

Once upon a time, on the Christian holy day of Sunday, and when the light was short in January—even in the subtropics of Texas, Child was born on a table of hard padded vinyl covered with green sterile sheets. He emerged between two branches of steel where Mother's feet rested. Overhead a huge surgical Light with three intensities and directional positioning looked down and called the Child good.

But Child, who whaa-ed out immediately and who was full of little arms and legs hurting for largesse and looking webbed momentarily at the elbows and knees until he stretched them out and pulsated his whole body a few times against this new thing called Time-and-Space—Child was even then planning how he would *be* in the world.

And he began by the teeny tiniest erection from the part of his body which had only seconds before served as the time-honored indicator of which one, male or female in the world, had increased.

Through this tiny upstanding protuberance, Child, no doubt frightened and excited as well as thinking futuristically, made his first overture to the world with a plume of amniotic fluid which his kidneys had been practicing on. It was portent of Child's unselfishness. The Doctor, however, did not immediately see Child's motive. Doctor, in fact, did not immediately see.

For this pure and innocent gift was hampered in its true trajectory by the face of Doctor, who was a silver-haired, no-nonsense woman of thick-lensed glasses long ago having faced many hardships in Nazi Germany and now temporarily unsympathetic to the goals of youth.

"How dare you make your entrance into this world by peeing in my face!" she scolded and handed him off, quarterback to receiver, who toweled Child summarily and laid him between the goalposts of his mother's breast.

So, from the beginning, Child was perplexed, to say the least. Because he had been thinking all along that World was a warm, wet, dark ride, a place for perfecting guitar licks and general frolicking. And instead, it was shiny, cold, hard, and had green sheets. It was a place where your gifts were rejected and you got passed around. Let us say that World failed, at least initially, to provide a proper nurturing environment for Child.

And the story would end here, and maybe Child would have turned out a social misfit because of the harshness of his first encounter with World, or maybe he would have sued Doctor for personal distress, pain, and suffering she caused in rejecting his first gift. Or maybe he would have divorced Parents for not providing therapy after the trauma of birth. Well, it could have been a serious ending indeed....

Except for the saving wisdom of Granddam, his father's mother. What she did so many years ago bestowed the charm of existence on Child and connected him to his home, the earth, and made him a lover of the natural world.

It seems that Mother's womb, for reasons of its own, was reluctant to surrender the idea of Child. (Who or what wouldn't be?—this child was so winsome.) And perhaps it was aided in its selfishness by the distraction of poor Doctor, blinded by Child's gift. At any rate, in a few days Child and Mother came home to the house set back in the orchard. And one evening, as she rose from the old wicker rocker after nursing Child, Mother left a wayward section of afterbirth which had been complaining bitterly all week that its Child was gone.

All this produced a great deal of excitement in the house and necessitated the need to return Mother to the place of chrome, plastic, and green sheets. Under Light, with three intensities and directional positioning, she was fixed, post-partum.

Suddenly, the cranky Doctor spoke. "Where is the afterbirth? I want to see this culprit." A call home was made, a questioning around of the ladies in waiting, and then Granddam stood up and answered, "It is gone. It now belongs to the coyotes."

For while the others had fixed a bottle of milk for Child and comforted him as best they could, and kissed the other children and put them to bed, Granddam had scooped up the mourning afterbirth and walked out into the countryside dark, all humid and a-breeze with the Gulf wind blowing inland, and flung it to the stars.

But gravity being what it was, the curious object fell among the aloes. And soon, as Granddam watched silently from the porch, it trotted with the coyotes through the mesquite, over the rise, in the direction of the Rio.

So that's how Child came to be the smiling sort, because his Granddam gave a little of him back to grit and grin that night.

And that's how Child got his today-but-yesterday wisdom, because he started out in high-tech chrome and plastic but got mixed in with the wicker chair and the wild dogs and the Rio.

The Greening of Souls

This morning I am repotting the bromeliads. There were three and now there are seven. Two were nearly the same size and I had to decide which one should be uprooted for the replanting, much like the parents of conjoined twins must decide about their separation.

The original mother plant of these three-now-seven was a gift from a bride, for my playing the flute at her wedding. Now she has been married several years and has just become a mother again. The placid darling child cooed and slept through church behind us a few Sundays ago. She has her babies; I have mine.

One of the two plants which were beginning to quarrel has produced a miraculous blossom for the last few years. Sometime in the early summer a single large pink bell-shaped flower appears out of the dark whorled center of the plant that acts as a reservoir for water. Inside this basic flower rises a nest of delicate red and blue flowerets. The concoction just sits there, impervious to time and weather, for some five months.

While I am transplanting—mixing possum smells and eggshells from our haphazard compost with pristine peat moss from the garden center—out of the corner of my eye I see a little pot swinging from the limb of the Texas laurel. It is a shabby neglected thing, now only a single string of five green round nubbins hanging over the side. I recall it was once a cascading hanging basket known as "string of pearls." My friend Barbara brought it to me one day when she came over to use our hot tub for her aching back.

Barbara is dead now. The pain in her back was a tumor on her spine, felling her in a matter of days after she came. The pool of Bethesda did her no good, not mine or any other water, though she had scores of loving friends to lift her in prayer.

But back to her plant. Slowly over the months, it has shriveled. The age-old enigma: too much or not enough sun and water? And I try now, in a final fit of sentiment, to think what to do to keep it alive.

I repot it, this time in eggshells, citrus bits, and possum pee. I water the scraggly green-pea jewels and say a blessing over them. Then I stand back a minute and notice what has occurred.

Here under this same tree are the remnants of life and death. A plant from a marriage, one that echoes the babies of that union in colors of pink, red, and blue. And a plant with a dubious future, borne to my yard by a dying friend.

Got to quit this silliness, I say aloud, fetching the watering can to sprinkle a few drops on Barbara's memory. What good does it do to attach my sadness, my heart's memories to a silly plant?

Twenty years ago I returned from the Mayo Clinic after a serious, life-saving surgery. One of our sons had waiting for me a cycad, known commonly as a sago palm, which he planted by the front porch. "This is a living thing, Mother; so are you." Through the years, I have taken that to mean that as that plant thrives, so would I. Rest assured I have given it lots of TLC. Today it stands taller than I, and the yardman has relieved it of countless suckers popping up at its base. Each year it produces a heavy pollen-covered male cone in its center, calling to the round seed-filled circle of the females nearby.

All these plants offer me the chance to continue my life. Green living things they are, charmed for now with the favors of sunlight and water. I long to preserve them so they will have some influence on me, the homeopathic effect. I shall be like them; they shall be like me.

We are bonded to things, especially for some of us, green living things. My sister recently found and clipped for me a story of an old woman willing her jade tree to her daughter. This tale of remembrance served to remind me, with alarm and urgency, of my grandmother's shatter rose bush. The original root stock has lived for 15 years in the yard of our mother. I called my sister, who lives in the same town as my late parents did. We have just put our parents' house on the market.

"You remember Mammaw's shatter rose bush? We've got to dig that up and transplant it before the house is sold." It will no doubt go into my sister's yard, with several cuttings coming home to South Texas in my carry-on luggage.

Joan Erickson, in her book *Wisdom and the Senses*, observes, "Things that we see and touch recall for us the loves and concerns, real or imagined, of those who touched and knew them well, valued and preserved them."

My sister and I will keep the shatter rose, a climber with small bright blossoms, as a way of keeping a piece of our grandmother, who had the brightest green thumb in Oklahoma. And with her memory, we will keep as well a piece of her daughter, our mother, who inherited the gardening trait with a will that kept everything she touched green and bearing, including the 100 African violets she insisted on cohabiting with in her assisted living apartment until she died at 93.

What will our children think to keep that we have loved and cared for? Their father's lime trees will be his legacy. For mine? Aloe veras and periwinkles are hardly rare enough. It must be something of age, valued in its own right for its stamina, beauty, or rarity.

Maybe my precious sago palm will outlive me, with palmlets galore continuing to come out of its base.

And when the house is sold (as surely it will be) I'll be there to haunt a son or daughter-in-law, waking them bolt upright some night to say, "Oh my gosh, we've got to get Mother's sago."'

Perhaps it won't be too late to write in a clause in the contract that says "all the landscaping *except the sago palm by the front door*...will remain."

Of course, they will have to summon a crew, and ball the roots, and get a front loader to deliver it across town to the local son's yard.

Something there is that would rather have my memory in a stubborn cycad than in a silver platter. Of course, I should be so lucky as to be remem-bered by a few artifacts—a loved blue vase, my childhood dolls, my Haynes flute. Certainly we return to dust, through ashes or no. But that dust is the food of living things.

If not my ghost hovering auspiciously in the heart of my sago, I still plan to be present. I'll be there in the form of extended family, my sister and brother cousins of dirt, eager to feed my memory.

Despite our age of rationality and disillusionment, we still live in a world of implicit charms, connections, graces. This plant is fertility. This one is my health. That one is gratitude.

www.ingramcontent.com/pod-product-compliance
Lightning Source LLC
Chambersburg PA
CBHW031238260626
47169CB00007B/2356